NETWORKING

for

FREELANCE
EDITORS

WORKBOOK

PRACTICAL STRATEGIES
for NETWORKING SUCCESS

BRITTANY **DOWDLE**

LINDA **RUGGERI**

First Edition, October 2021.

Published by the Insightful Editor (Linda Ruggeri) *theinsightfuleditor.com*

Copyediting by Word Cat Editorial Services
Proofreading by Madeleine Vasaly
Interior Design by Martin Publishing Services
Front Cover Design by Martin Publishing Services

ISBN-10: 1-7364205-0-8 (paperback), 978-1-7364205-1-5 (epub)
ISBN-13: 978-1-7364205-0-8

Library of Congress Control Number: 2021915331

Schools and Businesses: *Networking for Freelance Editors* is available at quantity discounts for bulk purchases for educational, business, sales, or promotional use. For information, please contact sales@networkingforeditors.com.

*To every freelance editor who needs to be reminded
that they're not alone, and that they will succeed.*

CONTENTS

FOREWORD

I t's hard to believe how much networking has changed over the years. There was a time that attending a networking event meant packing into small spaces with strangers. Holding a drink in one hand and business cards in the other. Mastering the art of small talk. And, more often than not, feeling rejected or out of place. These events were for the bold and extroverted, not the shy and introverted.

But as social media platforms continue to grow, and we've all had to adapt to increased online communication because of the pandemic, the idea of networking has taken on a new meaning. Gone are the days when traveling to a physical location was the only way to connect with others. We can now do this virtually, and this is welcome news for freelance editors in particular. Unlike entrepreneurs in other fields, editors don't always have the luxury or will to attend in-person networking events. Still, for social and professional reasons, we need to connect with others. But how do we show up with the right mindset? Take that first step?

Fortunately, Brittany Dowdle and Linda Ruggeri guide us through this process in their new book, *Networking for Freelance Editors*, a valuable resource for editors at any stage of their careers. Packed with personal anecdotes, worksheets, sidebars, and more, this book has a unique message: that, by giving back to the editing community—whether on a LISTSERV or Slack, via a retweet or a comment—we will make connections, immediately or in the future. Written in a warm, inclusive tone, *Networking for Freelance Editors* will appeal to all kinds of editors, regardless of their location or personality type. The advice Brittany and Linda provide for growing a network or building one from scratch is practical and actionable, and it can be applied right away.

Typically, editors encourage writers to find their voice in order to hone their craft. Brittany and Linda remind editors to find their voice in order to build their networks. As they say, our "unique voice is an essential part of our networking—it's our signature." I'll sign off on that.

Sangeeta Mehta
Developmental editor of trade fiction
Chair, Diversity Initiative, Editorial Freelancers Association
June 2021

INTRODUCTION

This guide is for editorial professionals who are new to editing, new to freelancing, or just not satisfied with their current network—whether that's because it's not a supportive community or because the hoped-for work opportunities haven't shown up yet. If you're a well-established freelance editor, chances are that you've built a network that's meeting your basic needs, and that's good! But we want to help you go beyond that and turn your network into something rich and dynamic—with resources and opportunities, with strong and meaningful contacts. We think you'll find a creative approach here that will help you build *new* business relationships—and opportunities.

Our purpose in writing this book is to help you create a networking practice that works for you—one that incorporates your goals, your communication style, the activities you enjoy, and the tools and resources that are available to you today.

Though networking may seem like an unwieldy, overwhelming task at times, we're going to show you that building the network you need is completely within your power, with the time and space available to you now. That network will be uniquely yours because it will be built on your goals, your strengths, and your everyday activities.

Our approach to networking is different from the compartmentalized style you may be used to—the one where you put on your "work" hat to work, your "marketing" hat to market, and your "networking" hat to network. In our experience as freelance editors, effective networking is all-encompassing—it's about making *connections*. This idea extends beyond simply connecting with other people; it means recognizing how everything you do as a freelance professional feeds into your ability to network effectively.

In this book, we're going to address aspects of your business that might traditionally be considered "not networking." But the fact is that in today's interconnected, social media–embedded world, none of us network in isolation. There *is* no specific "networking" hat. So, instead of treating networking as a discrete activity separate from your everyday workflow, we're going to show you that opportunities for networking are all around you. And you can harness these everyday activities to build your network naturally.

You might have noticed that we're not making a distinction between networking with other editors and networking with potential clients. Yes, there is a difference, but before we address that, we want to acknowledge that to a large extent, your different audiences will overlap—and they will each have access to the "you" you put out into the world. So, it's key to approach your networking through the expanded lens of social media marketing, content marketing, and website marketing, which is why we'll discuss these topics within the framework of business networking.

To network effectively today, we need to be *prepared* to network. And that is what much of this book is about: taking an integrated, whole-business approach to creating relationships and opportunities. To do this, we combine practical steps with a mindset that asks, *How can I contribute?* The practical steps identify *where* to network, and the generous mindset, unique to you as a freelance editor, shows you *how* to interact once you're there.

In our own research and experience, this approach has been continuously validated: effective networking is based on authentic relationships. And to build relationships, you have to be ready to give—of yourself, your wisdom, your empathy, your enthusiasm, your experience. Your greatest asset is that you have something the members of your network need (you), and by putting yourself in spaces where you can interact with them—whether virtually or in real life—you give yourself the opportunity to get to know and help others . . . and to be known and helped as well.

HOW TO USE THIS WORKBOOK

Networking for Freelance Editors is based on an interactive, step-by-step approach. There are two kinds of worksheets that we'll use throughout this book: self-assessment worksheets and the quarterly networking worksheet, which is a tool to help you set goals and implement your networking plan in a manageable way. Whether you're reading this as an ebook or in paperback, you can follow the links provided throughout the text and download copies of the worksheets from our website (www.networkingforeditors.com/resources).

We recommend printing them out and working through them as drafts (with a pencil or erasable pen) before settling on your final networking plan.

The steps that we'll cover in the following chapters include

- Understanding what networking is and why it's valuable

- Evaluating your current network and identifying opportunities for growth

- Determining your networking goals and whom you need to reach

- Exploring five networking tactics
  - Website
  - Personal communications
  - Social media
  - Professional groups
  - Volunteering

- Discovering your personal networking style

It doesn't matter whether you're a copyeditor, line editor, developmental editor, proofreader, book coach, fact-checker, or indexer. At the end of the day, our core networking goals are the same: to be part of a supportive professional community and to connect with clients we can help.

Are you ready to find networking opportunities in your everyday life? To create a sustainable plan that you can stick with? Be prepared, your first new networking step might be a cup of coffee at your local coffee shop to brainstorm with a fellow editor. Or attending an editorial association chapter meeting via Zoom. Maybe you'll be a guest blogger on someone's website, or create your own business posts on LinkedIn. The options are endless. That's an inspiring and frightening fact. The important thing is that you start doing what's comfortable for you (emphasis on the word *start*). This workbook is your guide for achieving tangible goals by making the most of your comfort zone and incrementally challenging yourself in your growth zone.

You can do it!

And we will be with you every step of the way!

GETTING TO KNOW EACH OTHER

Before we start connecting with others, we need to know *how to describe ourselves as professionals* and *how to frame our services*. Let us tell you a bit about ourselves; then you can share your "elevator introduction" using the following guide.

Brittany Dowdle

My name is Brittany Dowdle, and I'm a full-time book editor specializing in historical, mystery, and speculative fiction (SF/F) . . . and sometimes, the place where they collide. From my home in the north Georgia mountains, I provide copyediting for publishers, including Macmillan and Kensington; and for independent authors, I offer manuscript evaluations and developmental editing, with an emphasis on story craft. My pronouns are she/her.

Linda Ruggeri

My name is Linda Ruggeri, and I'm a full-service nonfiction editor based out of Los Angeles, specializing in developmental editing, line editing, and author coaching. I work with first-time authors, experienced authors, publishing houses (Hachette, Penguin Random House, the Cooking Lab), and small presses. My pronouns are she/her.

You

Now, tell us about yourself.

My name is _____

and I'm a/an _____ editor, specializing in _____.

I work with _____.
types of clients

I live in _____, and my pronouns are _____.
(if you're comfortable sharing them)

I'm ready to expand my network, help others, and grow my business.

My goals in reading this book are _____

_____

_____

_____

_____.

Now we can say, "Nice to meet you!"

We look forward to going on this networking journey together!

PART 1

REIMAGINING NETWORKING

The truth is that you've been networking all of your life with varying degrees of success—we all have. What's going to change today is *how* you think of networking. Together, we are going to reimagine networking.

CHAPTER 1

NETWORKING NOW

> *Networking is everywhere. Successful networking requires understanding the immense power of regular daily activities to connect with someone else.*
>
> —J. KELLY HOEY, BUILD YOUR DREAM NETWORK

Let's be frank. Many of us come to networking with a sense of dread. We think of it as transactional and potentially awkward. Though we've been told for years that networking is critical to our success, so much of what we know about it comes from the traditional business world, with its cleanly delineated, compartmentalized organizational charts and clear career paths. Meanwhile, as freelance professionals, we're in a "Create-Your-Own-Career" environment. Our needs are different. Our challenges are many. And we often lack access to the supportive infrastructure of a "regular" workplace, with its camaraderie, opportunities for mentorship, and built-in training and recognition processes.

When we're sitting (or standing) at our desks, trying to find the right clients, productive networking may seem like something that's beyond our reach. But what we've discovered is that as freelance professionals, we're in a unique position to network in an integrated, personalized way—one that's suited to the realities of our online and offline world. We just have to shift our perspective and make intentional use of the tools available to us.

WHAT IS NETWORKING?

At its core, **networking is behavior that builds a web of mutually beneficial relationships**. Like most relationships, our network is built over time, through everyday interactions—like being reliable, listening, keeping others' needs in mind, and reaching out to show support or give encouragement. These small actions reveal character, build connections, and create a space for us to get to know one another. And as our relationships grow, we find ourselves in an interlaced community that supports us and gives us opportunities to support others.

When we approach networking in this way, we realize that opportunities for networking are all around us. Later in this workbook, we'll dig deeper into what activities "count" as networking, but as a start, let's apply our definition of networking to various activities and consider how they measure up.

Networking is . . .

- offering insights with kindness and tact,
- helping clients connect with other editors if you aren't able to help them,
- maintaining long-term contact with colleagues and clients,
- answering questions from new editors or writers,
- sending former clients links related to their writing niches,
- sharing contest information or genre resources with authors, and
- sharing resources, relevant news, or job opportunities with fellow editors.

In other words, networking is building long-lasting professional relationships by sharing resources, expertise, and support.

Networking isn't . . .

- exchanging business cards, then dumping them in a drawer;
- ranting on forums;
- offering unsolicited grammar corrections;
- using your knowledge to put others down;
- asking others for their client lists;
- collecting random LinkedIn connections;
- expecting direct, tangible repayment for help you provide or referrals you make; or
- "emoji commenting," i.e., wholesale "liking" posts without commenting and engaging.

In other words, networking isn't transactional, impersonal, self-aggrandizing, or aimless.

If your idea of networking lines up with the first list, then you're off to a great start. But if the activities in the "Networking isn't" list look like the kind of networking you're familiar with, don't fret. Networking isn't something we learned in school. It can vary widely by culture, location, and industry. So, let's take this opportunity to reframe our thoughts around networking and explore how to network within the editorial freelancer's field.

We'll add our only disclaimer here: Our networking approach focuses on the positive and on giving back. Why? Because in our experience this is the type of networking that has the best results—both in terms of tangible success (often measured in client relationships) and in developing a professional support system. Networking not only grows our business, establishes lifelong working relationships, and increases our income. It can also provide us with emotional support and give us opportunities to socialize with like-minded people.

Networking Behaviors

Networking opportunities come in many forms, and while it's possible for some behaviors to fall squarely under "not networking" (we're looking at you, grammar peeving on Facebook), it's also possible for one activity to be either "networking" or "not networking" depending on whether we *engage* in it with a networking mindset and intentionality—or we just do it on autopilot.

Remember to use the definition "behavior that builds a web of mutually beneficial relationships" to test whether activities are worth investing in as part of a networking strategy. We find that framing this as a simple question keeps us mindful of our purpose, so we don't get overwhelmed or offtrack.

Next up is a basic networking mind map, or visual diagram, with some everyday activities. As we work through the following chapters, we'll explore these activities and how they serve us as networking touchpoints. For now, review this sample mind map and ask of each example activity, *How can this behavior help me build a web of mutually beneficial relationships?* If the connection isn't clear yet, that's okay. We still have much to discuss!

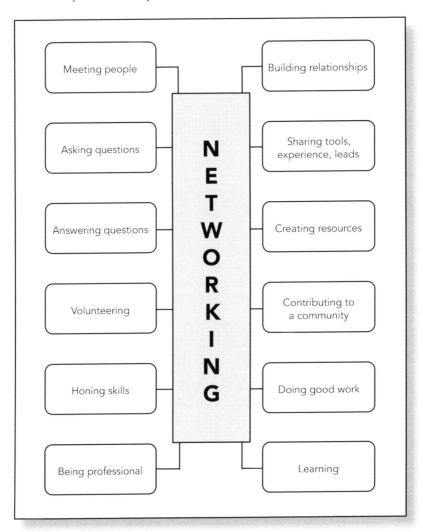

Sample networking mind map with possible networking activities.

Now use the following blank networking mind map to list activities that you think could be part of your networking plan. For each activity, ask the question, *How can this behavior help me build a web of mutually beneficial relationships?* If you don't have good answers yet, don't worry. The important thing here is to open our minds to the possibilities of what behaviors and activities can serve our networking today, as opposed to the tired old formula of yesterday. Once you've filled in at least six spaces, set the mind map aside.

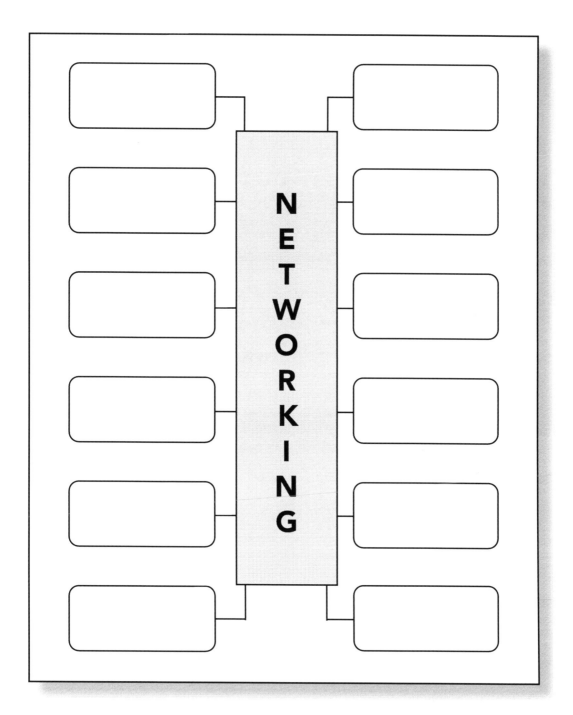

Practice networking mind map with possible networking activities.

In the following chapters, we'll explore how these (and other) activities work within a networking framework.

Altruism, good manners, and kindness always pay off.

—LINDA RUGGERI

AN EDITOR'S PERSPECTIVE

One of the things we should acknowledge is that networking can be uncomfortable for a lot of us. I know it is for me. Start small—you don't have to jump straight into attending networking events right at the start—and use social media to your advantage, especially sites like LinkedIn. Social media has made it so much easier to network because, as an introvert, I'm not fond of doing a lot of networking in person. Through social media, I can check up on how people are doing and send quick notes to say hi or congratulate them on a new job or on a publication.

—**ADAOBI OBI TULTON,** SERENDIPITY23 EDITORIAL SERVICES

CHAPTER 2

UNDERSTANDING YOUR NETWORK

To get the best, you must surround yourself with the most outstanding, caring, and helpful people.

—Rick Frishman and Jill Lublin, Networking Magic

At the time of writing this book, we are overcoming two exceedingly difficult years veiled under a long and trying global pandemic that has forced us to stop, to shelter, to wait—to wait even more—and to act mindfully not only for the sake of our own lives, but also for the sake of the lives of others.

For many of us, in order to cope and stay afloat, we've had to reach out and depend on new people—and be even more present for those close to us. We've discovered new ways to work, to adjust, to relate, and to keep going. We've built new networks without knowing it, reinforced other networks we had let dwindle, and treasured dearly the networks we can't live without. But we've also let go of networks that no longer served us, and that's a good thing too.

Who are these people we surround ourselves with in our daily lives (in person or virtually)? How do we relate to them? How do we support each other, and why does it matter? In this chapter, we're going to examine these connections and understand how they bring value to our lives as freelance editors.

THE TWO NETWORKS

As J. Kelly Hoey explains in *Build Your Dream Network*, there are two types of networks, and we need both to succeed.

The Small, Trusted Network

When the whole world is open to us through the internet, and when many editorial conferences are accessible by virtue of being online and therefore more affordable than in-person attendance, it may feel like our potential network is . . . everyone on the planet. Particularly for freelancers who are just starting out, there's a strong desire to connect with *anyone* who might be able to help us along our career path. But no matter where we are in our journey, we all need a primary safe space where we can share our experiences, both positive and negative, and learn from them. Quite often, this supportive environment isn't found in the wilds of cyberspace.

In everyday practice, we create this safe place by building a small, trusted network. Think of it as a networking home base. This close network usually consists of a few individuals we can go to with questions and doubts. It's where we discuss work challenges, share wins, refer clients, and offer support. The feedback we receive here really counts because it's coming from peers we trust and look up to, from mentors and colleagues who have our best interests at heart. These are the people we go to with questions that we might be uncomfortable asking in a large group—like on an international discussion list or a Facebook editors' group.

The small, trusted network is somewhere we can be vulnerable, where there's a good balance of give and take. In our experience, colleagues who are at similar places in their careers are often the best fit for this network because they are dealing with comparable issues and are invested in solving the challenges that crop up at that specific stage of the freelancing career. But it's also great to have a few more experienced connections in the small, trusted network, because they can act as mentors and guides. In turn, as we gain experience, we act as mentors for newer colleagues. **If you're a beginning editor or new to freelancing, work on building the close network first.**

It's in the small, close network that we have the opportunity for a deeper level of engagement and reciprocity so we can ask the hard questions, or give the hard feedback (in a kind way). Our small professional network is like a group of friends (a place of trust, dependability, listening), but it will always be exclusively related to our work as an editor (or indexer, or permissions checker, writer, proofreader, or designer). That said, in this network, we'll likely go beyond the usual professional-level interactions, supporting each other the same way we would take care of our friends—by checking in with them, sending them an occasional note or message, and celebrating their successes. It sounds a lot like friendship, right? But it isn't necessarily (though some people in this network may turn out to be friends too).

So, how do we build that close network?

As with networking in general, it takes time to build relationships. Places to start connecting with other editorial professionals are associations like ACES: The Society for Editing, the Chartered Institute of Editing and Proofreading (CIEP), the Editorial Freelancers Association (EFA), and Editors Canada, as well as Facebook groups (Louise Harnby's Training for Editors & Proofreaders, or the Business + Professional Development for Editors group) and the Editors Lair.

Don't be afraid to reach out to people whose posts are positive and friendly and introduce yourself. In particular, focus on people who share your editing niche (whether content or type of editing) or who are asking (or providing helpful answers to) the questions that are most pressing in your work. Rewarding business relationships and friendships often begin with the courage to reach out.

Another great way to connect with editors who are at similar places in their freelance careers is to take classes (in person or online) and get to know fellow students. While this is a bit harder for asynchronous classes (but can still be done), we've found that classes that have a group discussion component are excellent opportunities to expand and deepen our networks. How productive the discussion space is often depends on how well the instructor sets the tone and guides the conversation, so don't give up if one class doesn't further your networking goals. (Here we'll give a shout-out to Tanya Gold and Lourdes Venard, whose skills for community building make their classes great places to both learn and build relationships.)

Once you start building trusted, two-way relationships with individual editors, you may find there's so much knowledge and support being shared that you want to start connecting members of your network with each other. (Remember, just because it's a small network doesn't mean all the members know each other; it just means you know them because they are in your network.) And here's the great thing about this approach to networking—it spreads the benefits and builds community, instead of hoarding them and reinforcing isolation. Once you reach this point in your networking journey, you may be ready to consider forming a mastermind group, which is a cooperative group of peers who come together for growth, learning, and support. If this sounds intriguing, check out the next section for more about mastermind groups and how to create your own. Another option for those who prefer a one-on-one approach is to find a colleague you have a rapport with and become accountability partners.

Mastermind Groups

A mastermind group is a group of dependable people who share similar career objectives and work together to support each other in reaching those goals. Mastermind groups provide peer accountability, support, shared resources, inspiration, education, networking, and much more. The advantages of belonging to a mastermind group are many: it's a closed group; it's a safe place for developing long-lasting relationships built on trust; and it's made of colleagues you can rely on when you have questions and doubts, or need help finding resources.

As an example, our mastermind group started pretty organically, and it was definitely a result of good networking! Linda roomed with fellow editor Kellie M. Hultgren (whom she hadn't met before) at an editors' conference in Chicago a few years ago. A presenter discussed her participation in a mastermind group, which piqued Linda's curiosity. She mentioned it to Kellie, who had some resources about how to start one. Linda discussed it with Brittany to see whether she wanted in, and she did! Then Kellie reached out to Madeleine Vasaly, a colleague from the Professional Editors Network (PEN). And here we are, more than two years later, still meeting, still working on our goals—and with stronger businesses and happier professional lives because of it.

Through our mastermind group, we've learned a lot from each other. Above all, we've gained confidence in ourselves as editors. Confidence about when and how to say no to a client when the time frame, rate, or project doesn't suit us. Confidence about when and how to raise our rates. Or when to apply for that dream project we don't think we're good enough for (pushing back against our impostor syndrome). This mastermind group has taught each one of us why we are worth it.

There are many books and websites with suggestions for how to start a successful mastermind group, and for reference, we've listed some in appendix E.

In our experience, when setting up a mastermind group for freelance editors, it's best to

1. Keep it small. This way, each topic you're working on can be properly discussed, and each participant has time to share, as well as give feedback, or ask questions.

2. Keep your meetings organized. Use a preestablished agenda for each one (so you stay on track) with an *estimated* time to spend on each item. (For agenda structure ideas, see the end of this section.)

3. Be flexible. There are no set rules—only the ones you establish as a group. Choose the meeting topics according to what works for *your* group and what everyone is interested in achieving for themselves. Change, skip, or move agendas as you all see fit depending on the group's needs.

4. Set time limits. Other mastermind groups we know report that meetings usually run from one to two hours per session, and they meet every two or three weeks. This allows everyone enough time to follow through on the goals they are working on, or to research a discussion topic they can share with the group.

5. Remember, it's not a friendship (though it can turn into one). You don't have to be friends with or know everyone in your group when starting out. The idea is to surround yourself with editors who have different perspectives and experiences than you have, so you can learn about how others work, what works for them, what tools they use, what their experience is like, what their highs and lows are, and how they get through them. The perspective you gain from others will help you approach your own work challenges with new insights. It can also help you disengage from the stress of being wrapped up in your own head.

6. Be committed. You must commit to showing up—for the group, for the work, for yourself. It's okay if you have to miss a meeting (though often the group may choose to reschedule it), but make this group time a priority. Remember, it's time away from work that has the potential to produce income for you, so make it worthwhile.

7. Limit private-life sharing. We are freelance editors who hustle, who have families and responsibilities, and it's expected that life will get in the way. A mastermind group can become a safe space to share difficult problems you may be facing at work and, at times, in your personal life too. But be careful about oversharing or taking up too much time venting about your personal problems. This is not the place, and these are not the people for that. Yes, they are here to support you, but unless they specifically ask to know more, it's often a good idea to keep private matters private. As the group grows and you get to know each other more, there may be more space for sharing the personal stuff. (Note: We're not suggesting that anyone refrain from sharing out of a fear of stigma or because of self-censorship; rather, in our experience, it's important to cultivate safe spaces for personal sharing, and that's not necessarily a professional mastermind group. See our list of self-care resource links in appendix E.)

8. Be a good listener. Be mindful. Be open-minded, supportive, and encouraging. And walk away if the group is not for you, or for this time in your life. You can exit a group gracefully, with gratitude and goodwill. There's nothing wrong with realizing that it's not a good fit. Honoring your own boundaries and learning when to say no are important parts of successful networking (and freelancing). You can't say yes to every path, and trying to do so frequently leads to frustration.

When you start a mastermind group, it's good for each member to do a "business inventory," which is a snapshot of where they are in their business (similar to our quarterly networking worksheet) and where they want to be by year's end. Members share this information with the group and devise individual steps (or building blocks) that will contribute to each goal. Once everyone has established their goals and intermediate steps/strategies, the group can schedule regular quarterly (or weekly, or monthly) goal reviews where everyone checks in and shares what they've accomplished so far—and what they still have on their to-do lists.

Though this sounds like a streamlined process, depending on how much time the group has and the approach that makes sense for the members, it's possible that much of the early self-assessment, goal setting, and strategizing might be done as a group, with a lot of back-and-forth and opportunities to give and get feedback. This is particularly helpful for newer editors. Other mastermind groups might have more experienced members who are set on their goals and next steps and who really just need accountability partners. Discussing and setting expectations before embarking on the group mastermind journey will help everyone get on the same page and make sure their communication and learning styles mesh.

Here's a sample of what our meeting agenda looks like:

1. News or successes since last call

2. Progress report on goals from last call

3. Discussion topic of the week (e.g., three top-priority goals, or a review of project management software that we use, or webinars we are taking/books we are reading for continuing education)

4. Requests for backup (e.g., asking for support or reality checks)

5. Set time for next call

LINDA'S PERSPECTIVE

Our mastermind group has been invaluable in helping us grow as editors and as business owners. At one point I shared that I was struggling with a client who didn't communicate clearly and was always changing their mind, setting the project's publication date further and further along, which didn't allow me to work on other projects. But they paid on time and paid my rate. The project was completed, the book got published, and that was that. But, four months later, the author approached me again for a separate project. And I considered it.

I consulted with my mastermind group, sharing my doubts, and they each reminded me of all of the things I had complained about when working on the first project and what a headache it had been. They wisely said that if I booked that work, it would prevent me from picking up other projects I'd be excited to work on. They reminded me how unreliable the author was about turning in their best work, and how most of the time the author didn't listen to the editorial advice I offered. Was it really worth my emotional health and time?

My mastermind partners were right. I trusted their opinion and knew that if they were telling me this, it was because they had seen me in the thick of it and knew how frustrated I was. They knew I could book better work than that. I ended up gracefully bowing out of the project and referring the author to three different editorial directories where they could post their project or look for another qualified editor. And even when I dropped that client, other work continued to come in, and I was able to focus my attention on the type of editing I wanted to do.

Lesson: I needed that small network to keep me in check, to show me I had other options.

The Broad, Dispersed Network

If our small, trusted network gives us depth and substance, the broad, dispersed network gives us reach. There will be overlap between our small and broad networks, but we can distinguish between them by focusing on how we'll interact with each group and the kind of benefits we'll give and potentially receive depending on the nature of the network. Here are a few metaphors that help us visualize how these two networks function.

For instance:

- The small network is a coral reef; the broad network is the entire Pacific Ocean.
- The small network is a solar system; the broad network is the universe.
- The small network is immediate family; the broad network is the massive family reunion.

Can you add a metaphor that helps you conceptualize how these networks function—and your place in them?

This expanded network consists of people we may only know online—people we follow and interact with on a larger, less personal level (like peers on a discussion list, a subject matter expert we just found on Instagram, a prominent author on Facebook, a managing editor on Twitter). We're able to relate to them because we share common goals and are in a similar industry (or industries that complement each other), but we don't know the person in real life and haven't had extensive communication with them online.

This loosely connected network is made of individuals—and communities—we interact with without being particularly intimate or vulnerable—it's a wider net of diverse contacts. Yes, they are more superficial at first—because we haven't developed relationships yet—but they enrich our perspective and also give us a chance to make connections beyond our everyday relationships. As we get to know members of this broad network, we'll look for opportunities to deepen our exchanges and perhaps meet offline—at conferences, for coffee, or in other meetups. And if we're networking with the goal of gaining new clients (not all of us are), *the more people who know that we're an editor, the better.*

This extended network is a great place to both learn and teach (in other words, share our knowledge and build our reputation for expertise—and approachability). While our close network mainly consists of people we have much in common with, the wide network is where we go to expand our boundaries or to conduct research that's beyond the perspective of our immediate network. Just as freelance editing can be isolating, at times the editing community can be insular. Reaching out beyond our usual sources of information helps us stay informed, open-minded, and inclusive. And for a freelance professional, these qualities are critical to success.

AN EDITOR'S PERSPECTIVE

Networking seemed somewhat unnecessary to me from the relative security of a full-time job for a publishing company in Mexico. But jobs don't last forever, and personal priorities change: organizing your agenda, being your own boss, spending more time on the things that matter to you, and, yes, starting from zero when a pandemic devastates the economy and takes away "nonessential" businesses. My search for new horizons in the United States—a market with sixty million Spanish speakers—led me to various associations for publishing professionals, and as an international member of the Editorial Freelancers Association, I discovered the value of networking: sharing experiences, knowledge, and projects with other editors. Without being a full-time freelance editor yet, I realized the importance of stepping out of the full-time employee comfort zone.

—Luis Arturo Pelayo, Spanish to Move

INSIGHT: NOTES ON AUDIENCE

As we mentioned earlier, for much of this workbook we don't make a distinction between networking with editorial peers and networking with potential clients. Today especially, so many of our interactions are public—or publicly available—that targeting specific audiences with specific messages can be difficult. There's a lot of overlap, and it's especially important to present a cohesive brand presence, regardless of your audience.

For this reason, we recommend that editors be circumspect with how they present themselves and how they talk about clients, competitors, and peers in virtual and real-life spaces. There are places and times that are appropriate for venting or sharing potentially embarrassing information, such as in a secure space with close, trusted colleagues. But remember that the world at large isn't a safe space. There are trolls and others who will judge harshly and harass freely simply because they can, because it feeds the less-pleasant instincts of human nature. And there are potential clients who don't need to know their editor's particular life circumstances, unless the editor chooses to share the information with them. Our point here is, be *intentional* about what you share. And keep in mind that *intended* audience is not the same as *actual* audience.

Figuring out how open or private to be online, especially as a freelancer, is a challenging and personal decision. What works for some of us won't work for others, so we're not going to give specific recommendations beyond what we've said already. (But for an insightful discussion on finding your own balance, read the article "Too Much Information, or Not Enough?" by Liz Jones of Responsive Editing. See appendix E.)

Another consideration regarding audience is deciding what information and assistance to give away without charging for it (as when mentoring a newbie or helping a member of a close network), and what constitutes billable work. As with most everything freelance, this is a personal business decision. As part of our community mindedness, we'll often spend a fair amount of time helping peers (with résumés, figuring out how to deal with difficult clients, researching technical questions, etc.), but we've found that when dealing with clients, it's often wise to be diligent about boundaries, especially where project scope and fair compensation are concerned. In each case, regardless of who the audience is, it's important to remember that relationship building is the foundation of networking, and to build real relationships, it's necessary to be honest, set expectations, and maintain healthy boundaries.

BRITTANY'S PERSPECTIVE

In our everyday lives it can be easy to compartmentalize relationships and networks (these are my neighbors, these are my clients, these are my editing colleagues, these are my hometown friends, these are my cat rescue fellow volunteers, these are my organic gardening friends, etc.). Mental divisions like these are often natural because people like to categorize information and group people/things according to their similarities. That's okay. But it's important to remember that just because someone is not in your "client" group today does not mean they are not a potential client for tomorrow.

Some of my most rewarding projects have come through members of my extended network who knew me, knew my work ethic, and knew that I was an editor. They referred me to their friends (and employers), trusting that I would help them if I could, or at least point them in the right direction if we weren't a good fit.

The takeaway is that you have a huge potential network of people who know you. Make sure they also know what you do. When you mention your work, let your enthusiasm come through, speak well of your clients, share your successes. You don't need to be a nonstop self-advertisement, but do take pride in your work and mention it when people ask what you're up to or what's new. Make it easy for your extended network to remember that they have a friend in publishing—you!

EVALUATE YOUR CURRENT NETWORK

How do we decide where to find our broad network connections? That's coming up in chapter 3: Networking Goals. But first, let's use the worksheets at the end of this chapter to evaluate our starting point: the small/trusted and broad/dispersed networks we have right now.

Think about who is currently in each network, and whom you would like to have in your network. Is your trusted network solid, but do you seldom venture out of it? Or are you in all the places, meeting all the people, while sensing that what you really need are a few trusted colleagues you can talk to with a greater degree of openness?

Use the following exercise to help visualize your current networks, so you can gain perspective and have a better idea of the nature and depth of your web of professional relationships *today*. After all, to form a plan for where we want to go (and how to get there), we must first know where we're starting out.

In the worksheets, make note of

People: Whom are you interacting with? (People are key because relationships are key!)

Platform: What medium do you interact with them on? (Text messaging? Slack space? Email? Twitter? Local chapter meeting? Conference? Phone? Zoom? Instagram? LinkedIn? Facebook?)

Industry: What area do they work in (which is, hopefully, an industry that you draw business from)? This might be a specific community (indie contemporary romance authors, PhD candidates in the social sciences, corporate HR clients, niche academics, military memoirists, self-help authors, thriller writers) or a particular specialty within the publishing industry (acquisitions editors, cover designers, permissions editors, technical editors, book coaches, translators, book launch specialists, formatters, indexers, sensitivity readers).

After you fill out the following worksheets,* take a few minutes to evaluate what you find. Do most of your close connections come from a single source—a previous employer, a specific professional organization, a niche editing Facebook group? If so, what benefit might there be in cultivating strong relationships with people outside those groups (not to replace your trusted network, but to broaden it)?

For instance, if most of your close connections are from a previous in-house job, that's probably a comfortable, safe space—and possibly a great source of business. But sudden changes in that company's management or direction might leave you floundering, especially if your close network is too narrow. By putting your current networks (small *and* broad) on paper, you can identify patterns and gaps that might not stand out otherwise.

Take this opportunity to find both the strengths and the areas for improvement (via expansion or deepening) in your current network. Maybe there are types of contacts you're missing and need to add. (For example, if you're an editor who works mainly with indie authors, you'll be able to better serve your clients if you can offer trusted recommendations for cover designers, virtual assistants, or beta readers.) When considering your broad, dispersed network, in particular, don't underestimate the many connections you already have. Part of being a successful freelancer is finding opportunities in the unlikeliest of places.

---

* Keep in mind that the worksheets throughout this book provide snapshots of where you are today and will evolve as you develop your networking strategy. You'll revisit them as you continue to develop your strategy and abilities. Ideally, you'll be filling out a quarterly networking worksheet (see chapter 3) four times a year and revisiting these self-assessment worksheets when needed to help you gain clarity and perspective. And remember, there are no wrong answers!

CURRENT NETWORK SNAPSHOT

Date: _____

MY SMALL, TRUSTED NETWORK

My current small, trusted network is made up of the people listed below. I know I can go to them with questions, doubts, ideas, or success stories, and that I will receive their honest feedback.

PERSON	PLATFORM	INDUSTRY/SPECIALTY REPRESENTED

Questions: Whom is my network missing?
What does this tell me about my preferred platform?
Am I networking exclusively in one niche?

CURRENT NETWORK SNAPSHOT

Date: _____

MY BROAD NETWORK

My current broad network is made up of the people listed below. I may not know all of these connections personally, but they are in my orbit and help broaden my understanding and reach.

PERSON	PLATFORM	INDUSTRY/SPECIALTY REPRESENTED

Questions: Whom is my network missing?
What does this tell me about my preferred platform?
Am I networking exclusively in one niche?
Is my network shallow and disjointed?

Place the worksheets side by side and notice how they compare. Are your two networks balanced in terms of the number of contacts and the industries represented? Or is your overall (combined) network shallow and disjointed? Is the focus too narrow? Too broad? Make some preliminary notes and hold on to these worksheets. We'll revisit them in chapter 10.

For those who prefer a spatial/visual approach, you might try using the mind map method instead of the list worksheets. Here's an example of how to map your broad network, with some starter connections.

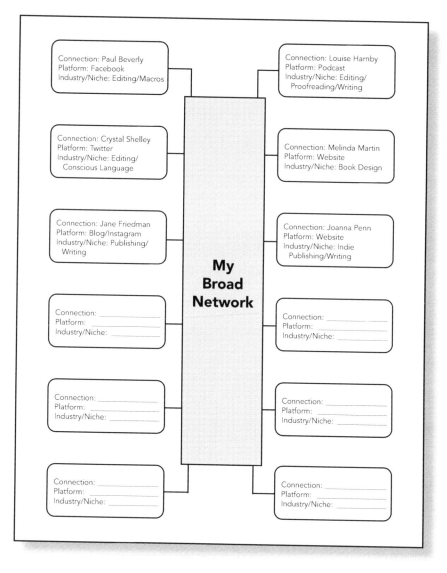

Broad network practice mind map.

After you've filled out these snapshots (or constructed your network mind maps) and have a better understanding of your current networks, move on to chapter 3, where we'll work on developing your networking goals. Then we'll dive into chapter 4, where we'll identify whom you need to reach as you pursue those goals.

CHAPTER 3

NETWORKING GOALS

> *The best way to overcome our resistance to networking is to clarify our networking goals. Then, have a "WIN" attitude. Identify "What's Important Now."*
>
> —BRITTANY DOWDLE & LINDA RUGGERI

Why network?

Short answer: to help us achieve our goals and find solutions to our challenges.

The accepted wisdom is that networking is something we should all be doing. It's touted as a magic key in advice like "It's not what you know, it's who you know." But often we approach this important activity with unfocused intentions and an unclear understanding of how to do it "right" and how it will help us. The line between effort and return on investment is nebulous at best.

Though we know networking is something we're *supposed* to do, many of us are uncomfortable when it's time to actually get out there and "network." This discomfort may come from social anxiety, or from the dread of being viewed as pushy or characterized as trying to "monetize" our relationships. And since some of us have complicated feelings around money—and seeking clients (going after business)—these can also compound our discomfort.

As freelancers who mostly work at home by ourselves, we also run the risk of living in a thermos. We lock ourselves up in our own little space, solely interact with a screen (or two), maybe even our cats or dogs, and clatter away at our keyboard all day. It's a safe haven; it's what we know; it's where eight hours can go by in the blink of an eye. But it's also isolating, and we can quickly lose touch with reality, with new industry trends, with the big picture. It's easy to become hyperfocused and neglect our place in the editing community. And when that happens, we can miss out on work opportunities, on catching up with colleagues, on learning about classes or conferences—or even on meeting new clients who are looking for someone with our skills to edit their work.

These everyday stresses and habits contribute to our internal resistance to effective and mindful networking. Think of resistance as the little voice that says, *I don't have time to network. Is it really worth it? No one's interested in my perspective—I don't have anything interesting to share, etc.* Resistance is challenging for anyone, and because we're freelancers, we have to push ourselves through it and be our own advocates to ensure we're doing the sometimes-uncomfortable work that keeps us relevant and connected.

To counter these obstacles to effective networking, the first step we'll take in this chapter is to **identify what we want to accomplish with our networking**. In other words, What is the *goal* networking can help us achieve? Why network?

Having measurable, well-defined goals will focus our efforts so we can network with intention. When we identify these goals (our destination), networking becomes the path between where we are today and that destination. (But remember, the destination we're working toward isn't the final stop on our professional journey—it's simply the next step.)

We'll start by reviewing some of the main reasons freelance editors network. At the bottom of the following list, we've added a few extra bullet points for you to fill out in case we've missed goals that are important to you. (If you notice that some of these goals are overlapping, you're right. Welcome to freelance life!)

Freelance editors network . . .

- to build long-term client relationships
- to build long-term colleague relationships
- to get more clients
- to diversify our client portfolios (and keep our work interesting)
- to establish a reputation
- to build a brand
- to increase revenue through new opportunities
- to be part of a community
- to learn from colleagues
- to help colleagues (by sharing what we know)
- to be part of the conversation and stay relevant
- to improve our skills
- to develop new skills
- to stay informed of industry best practices
- _____
- _____

Which of these goals are most important to you *at this point in your professional journey?*

In case the list is too overwhelming—you probably want to accomplish all of these goals right now—let's meet some editors who also need to identify their most pressing business needs (a.k.a. goals) and how networking can help them succeed.

Editor Snapshot (Needs and Goals)

Meet Ana, the new-to-editing editor:

Ana has just started her freelance editing business after completing a certificate program, and her goal is **to get more indie clients (focusing on mystery genre)**, so she decides to focus on **establishing her reputation** and **building her brand**. Many other excellent reasons for networking may feed into her primary goal, but she can't do everything at once, so she's decided to focus on this multipart goal.

Ana's main goal: get more indie mystery clients who need copyediting and proofreading

Ana's building-block goals:

- establish a reputation
- build a brand

Meet Joy, the new-to-freelancing editor:

Joy has worked in-house, but now she's going freelance, and the transition is stressful. She already has some great connections in publishing, but she needs to learn more about the business side of freelancing, so Joy's networking goal is **to build a successful freelance career** by **learning business best practices from colleagues** and **establishing a freelance reputation**.

Joy's main goal: build a freelance career

Joy's building-block goals:

- learn freelancing business skills
- establish a freelance reputation

Meet Taylor, the established editor trying to increase their income:

Taylor has built a satisfying career, but they need **to be more profitable**. This might mean new income streams, working more efficiently, or changing their mindset around money. There are so many possibilities, but they're going to have to narrow their focus. Taylor is in a stable place financially, so they decide to take their time and network with other editors to find out how others have met this challenge.

Taylor's main goal: be more profitable

Taylor's *possible* building-block goals:

- identify new income streams (coaching, classes, workshops, presentations, etc.)
- change money mindset (raise rates, etc.)
- learn more efficient editing practices
- change editing niche

Meet Alex, the fatigued editor:

Alex has plenty of work and a solid reputation in his niche, but he's feeling isolated and stuck in his specialty. He needs to **get out of his rut and into a more positive headspace**. Alex's networking goals are **to diversify his client portfolio** and **to become part of a community**, so he has more support from editors who "get" him and can help him navigate the emotional stresses of his work.

Alex's main goal: get out of his rut and into a more positive headspace

Alex's building-block goals:

- diversify his client portfolio
- become part of a community

Your Editor Snapshot (Needs and Goals)

Take a moment to evaluate your own situation. Do you identify with Ana, Joy, Taylor, or Alex? Or is your situation a bit different?

Without overthinking it, quickly fill out the following, placing yourself in the role of one of our editors:

Your Editor Snapshot (Needs and Goals)

Meet _____ **, the** _____ **editor:**
                    your name   *adjective*

I have _____ **, but** _____.
         current situation/experience   *unmet need/challenge*

To meet this need/fix this problem/change this situation, my goal is

_____

_____

_____

_____

_____

_____

_____.

To achieve this goal, I will focus on these building-block goals (list two networking goals that have the potential to solve this challenge):

_____

_____

_____

_____

Now, set this aside for a moment and read on.

Setting Goals

Without a clear goal, our networking efforts are often inefficient and draining. We may eventually arrive at our destination, but the journey will likely take longer and be fraught with wrong turns and dead ends. At times we'll run out of gas, causing us to lose motivation and default to simply going through the networking motions. (Hello, drawer full of abandoned business cards! Goodbye, TikTok account that we signed up for and never used!)

When our networking goals are undefined and our actions aren't moving us closer to achieving our aims, we've found that a good approach is to take a step back and make our goals *overt and specific*. That way, we're in a better position to develop a solid, actionable plan instead of the usual scattered-pasta-against-the-wall plan so many of us default to while hoping for the best.

Whose Goals?

The first step when linking goals to our networking plan is to realize that our goals are unique and will change over time. Even though we're all editorial professionals, we don't all have the same goals. Why? Because we edit in different genres and niches—with different specialties and skill sets. Because each one of us is at a different place in our career. Because we all have different responsibilities, needs, and life situations.

Some of us are just starting off in our editing careers, while some of us are midcareer, and others may be looking for a change of industry or clients. Some are looking to retire within a year and would like to work part-time, maybe changing their niche to align with their hobbies. Because we are individuals, our goals are different, and the beauty of networking is that no one goal or strategy applies to everyone. We get to set our goals and customize our path based on what works for us—based on what *need* we're working to fulfill today.

Let's take a moment to digest that idea: another person's goal may not fit *our* situation. It follows that the networking tactics they employ might not be the best choice for *our* goals. It's easy to be seduced by the shiny, sparkling wonder of someone else's goal-strategy journey. *They have it all figured out*, we think. *I just have to do everything they're doing, then I'll have made it.* To that, we say: By all means, study other people's success, study their methods, analyze what resonates, and examine why it's working (e.g., their volunteer work builds community, their blog posts establish reputation/brand, their LinkedIn articles show their subject matter expertise). But always come back to your goals and base your networking plan on what *you need* to build the career *you* want.

Pause and give yourself permission to do some deep thinking about where your business is and where it's headed. Though foundational goal development is beyond the scope of this workbook, we want to emphasize that your networking strategy needs to be based on your business goals for it to be efficient and deliver the intended results. We've provided some additional resources in appendix E that can help you with goal setting. In the meantime, start where you are—follow your instincts and craft the starter goals that will move you in your intended direction.

Goal Time

Using the editor-snapshot exercise as a starting point, brainstorm the business goals that will help you get to the next level in your freelance career. There may not be one right answer, but rather a few serviceable answers that you must choose between.

Beginning from a macro level, jot down your main goal, and then brainstorm a few building-block goals that will help you achieve the main goal. For each goal that you set, ask yourself, *Is this goal measurable, achievable, and dependent on my own actions?*

If you're a visual thinker, use this template.

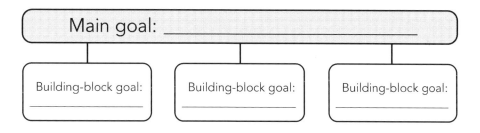

Blank networking goals mind map.

For example, here's Joy's goal map:

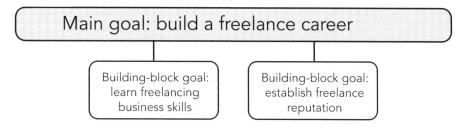

Joy's networking goals mind map.

Goals

Next, use the space provided to elaborate on your main and secondary goals for your business.

My main goal for this year is: _____

_____

_____

_____

_____

_____

_____

My building-block goals (designed to support my main goal) are: _____

_____

_____

_____

_____

_____

_____

Goals should be broad enough to give you room to grow, but narrow enough to give you direction—and a way to objectively evaluate whether you've hit them.

BRINGING IT ALL TOGETHER: THE QUARTERLY NETWORKING WORKSHEET

Now that you've established your top business goals, you can begin to fill out the quarterly networking worksheet by inserting these goals into the first section. The purpose of condensing your networking plan into one sheet is to give you a high-level summary that you can print out and keep close by. This worksheet is important because it will help you

- organize your thoughts,
- create a plan,
- position yourself to get results, and
- evaluate your successes at the end of each quarter.

As we work through the following chapters, we'll continue to fill out this worksheet, but for now only complete the first section (main goal, building-block goals, and start date).

QUARTERLY NETWORKING WORKSHEET

Start Date:

_____

Main Goal:

Building-Block Goals:

👤 **Based on my networking goal(s) for this quarter, whom do I need to reach now?**

👤 **How can I use each Networking Tactic to reach them?**

Action for My Website:

Action for My Personal Communications:

Action for My Social Media:

Action for My Professional Organizations:

Action for My Volunteer Activities:

END-OF-QUARTER NETWORKING REVIEW

End Date:

_____

Progress:

Editor Check-In:

If you'd like to see how our three other colleagues completed their sheets, head over to our website for additional ideas (www.networkingforeditors/resources). There you will also find our own lists of business goals for the year.

For now, here's how Ana filled out the first section of her worksheet:

QUARTERLY NETWORKING WORKSHEET

Start Date:
October 1, 2021

Main Goal:
get more indie clients

Building Block Goals:
establish reputation and build brand

AN EDITOR'S PERSPECTIVE

For me, there are several different outcomes I want to achieve by networking with my fellow editors. I want to:

- Be known—so I'm top of mind if someone needs to make a recommendation or referral.
- Learn about others—so I can be the one making referrals and recommendations.
- Learn from others—since there's always so much to learn about running an editorial business.
- Make friends with people who understand my profession—so I can moan about commas to people who understand my pain!

If I have referrals and recommendations coming in, if I know whom to recommend if I can't take on a job myself, if I'm able to tap into the collective wisdom of my industry, and if I feel like I've made some friends along the way, that all feels like the result of successful networking.

—**SOPHIE PLAYLE**, LIMINAL PAGES

CHAPTER 4

USING GOALS TO IDENTIFY POTENTIAL NETWORKING PARTNERS

Your network is your net worth.

—PORTER GALE, AUTHOR AND ENTREPRENEUR

People tend to work with, and refer work to, people they know and trust. So the first networking step is *becoming known*, and the second is *building trust*. Before you can do either, however, you need to identify whom your ideal network is composed of—and where they can be found.

But there's no reason to feel overwhelmed, because you've already identified your primary goals and the building-block goals in the last chapter. Now you can use those goals to determine whom you need to reach and where you can find these future networking partners. Take a look at your Self-Assessment Worksheets: Current Network Snapshot from chapter 2 (p. 25).

Does your combined network contain the people you need to connect with in order to reach your specific goals?

If not, it might be time to broaden your network or pursue a more specialized cohort of connections. Notice, we're not saying to drop current contacts based on whether they are useful to you—that's transactional and contrary to maintaining real relationships. We are saying that if your network is a mismatch for the direction you're trying to move in, then you need to expand your network in the direction of your desired growth. But keep those early connections! If you have a rapport with someone, don't squander it. Tomorrow's networks are built of yesterday's and today's relationships. And keep in mind that a significant part of networking is being there for others—being a strong support in someone else's network. That spirit of selfless support and giving is at the core of every effective networking relationship.

Editor Snapshot (People to Connect With)

Let's revisit our four editors to see whom they might want to develop relationships with based on their goals:

Ana, the new-to-editing editor:

Ana's main goal: get more indie mystery clients who need copyediting and proofreading

Ana's building-block goals:

- establish a reputation
- build a brand

Ana needs to connect with (general): mystery writers who need editing services; editors who can offer community, learning opportunities, and referrals. Where are they active?

Ana needs to connect with (specific): indie author community within mystery genre; editors who specialize in working with indies—in particular, those who offer complementary levels of editing, such as developmental editing; organizations that support indie authors; Facebook groups where indie authors congregate to discuss craft; professional editing associations; bloggers who curate writing resources for writers. Where are they active?

Joy, the new-to-freelancing editor:

Joy's main goal: build a freelance career

Joy's building-block goals:

- learn freelancing business skills
- establish a freelance reputation

Joy needs to connect with (general): publishers who need editing services, freelance editors who can offer community and share experiences (and lessons learned). Where are they active?

Joy needs to connect with (specific): professional editing associations, informal editing groups (perhaps on Facebook), freelance communities (like the Freelancers Union), instructors specializing in the business of editing, SCORE (the Service Corps of Retired Executives), production editors with various publishers. Where are they active?

Taylor, the established editor trying to increase their income:

Taylor's main goal: be more profitable

Taylor's *possible* building-block goals:

- identify new income streams (coaching, classes, workshops, presentations, etc.)
- change money mindset (raise rates, etc.)
- learn more efficient editing practices
- change editing niche

Taylor needs to connect with (general): editors at similar stages of their careers, editors in other niches, editors who are open to new ways of practicing their craft. Where are they active?

Taylor needs to connect with (specific): professional editing associations, productivity specialists (in editing and in freelancing), mindset coaches, editors who use platforms or products like Dubsado (customer relationship manager) or ConvertKit (mailing list manager), editors in related niches that might be more profitable, editors who offer coaching, online classes, etc. Where are they active?

Alex, the fatigued editor:

Alex's main goal: get out of his rut and into a more positive headspace

Alex's building-block goals:

- diversify his client portfolio
- become part of a community

Alex needs to connect with (general): clients who need his specific specialty, but whose business model or content is different from his current client roster; clients who are in adjacent industries; clients who offer short projects with quick turnaround times, as opposed to current clients who have massive projects; editing groups. Where are they active?

Alex needs to connect with (specific): niche industry groups whose members are potential clients; editing organizations and groups that have community-minded goals (like the EFA's Diversity Initiative), where Alex can get to know others, interact, and share his knowledge; editing groups with peers who are at similar points in their careers or who share Alex's specialty. Where are they active?

As these examples show, different editors may develop relationships with widely divergent groups based on their specific goals. Academic editors will need to reach different kinds of clients and colleagues than translators, who will need different connections than romance editors, who will need an altogether different network than indexers or writers. And even within the broader content genres, each editorial professional may need to network in distinctive ecosystems. For instance, the networking plan of a thriller proofreader is going to differ from that of a developmental editor who specializes in grimdark fantasy.

But we'll also have some overlap, generally in industry groups like ACES: The Society for Editing or in Facebook editing groups. In our experience, these large groups are great places to start, but many of our most valuable connections will be found in the smaller niche groups where we can really get to know people and form relationships. This is true for developing both industry connections and potential clients. So, our recommendation is to begin with the wide groups, then, through daily and weekly interaction, start to build relationships with people who have similar interests, specialties, skill sets, and goals. (More on this in chapter 6.)

Once you identify whom you'd like to have in your network (in general or specific people/roles), then you can work on becoming known (a.k.a. using your website and social media for networking purposes, for example) and building trust (a.k.a. helping others find their own answers, sharing your knowledge, encouraging others).

Your Editor Snapshot (People to Connect With)

Try this exercise yourself, using the information from your earlier editor snapshot:

👤 *Your Editor Snapshot (People to Connect With)*

Meet _____ **, the** _____ **editor:**
               your name   *adjective*

_____**'s main goal:** _____
    your name

_____

_____

_____**'s building-block goals:**
    your name

- _____

    _____

- _____

    _____

👤 **People to connect with (general):**

_____

_____

_____

👤 **People to connect with (specific):**

_____

_____

_____

👤 **Where they are active:**

_____

_____

_____

👤 **Where they are active:**

_____

_____

_____

Spend some time brainstorming who can help you reach your current goals. Look past the obvious choices and get creative. Come back to the list and let your mind wander. You can always dial back your reach, but start by giving yourself the space to imagine whose insights you'd love to have. Who is an expert in your desired niche? Who is your dream client? Write down names, organizations, conferences, and social media hangouts.

For example, maybe, like Ana, you want to work with more indie authors of fiction. First jot down a category (indie authors), then narrow it down (indie authors who write mystery), then get specific (indie mystery authors who are members of Sisters in Crime or who participate in a Facebook mystery authors group), then identify a few leading indie mystery authors and write down their names. Add them to your quarterly networking worksheet under the question *Based on my networking goal(s) for this quarter, whom do I need to reach now?*

A quick note: It's not that you're going to email every best-selling indie mystery author and ask to be their best friend. You *are* going to follow them online, see where they hang out, what author groups they interact with, what's important to them. And as you get a feel for that community of indie mystery authors, you'll begin to interact and contribute—first as a learner, then offering your own insights. You can be up-front and honest about your position (as a mystery editor), but also show your desire to learn from the group. This type of networking can build your genre knowledge base, help you create a reputation (for example, as an editor who provides resources for beginning mystery writers), and enable you to understand your target clients' expectations and needs. In turn, developing this networking practice can help you gain more indie clients by

1. establishing your reputation as a knowledgeable and approachable freelance editor, and

2. building your brand and positioning yourself as an expert within your genre or specialty.

Of course, this is an abbreviated version of the networking process, but once you fill out the next section of your quarterly networking worksheet, you'll be ready to move on to the next chapters, which focus on the specific networking tactics that form the structure of your networking plan.

Quarterly Networking Worksheet

Transfer your list of potential contacts from your editor snapshot on page 45 into the quarterly networking worksheet.

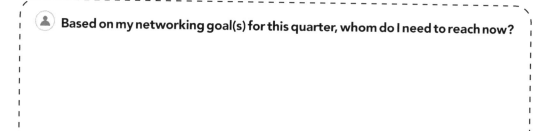

Based on my networking goal(s) for this quarter, whom do I need to reach now?

Editor Check-In:

As an example, here's Ana's first attempt at identifying whom she needs to reach:

 Based on my networking goal(s) for this quarter, whom do I need to reach now?
1. Indie mystery authors (in FB groups, Sisters in Crime, other writing groups)
2. Developmental editors who need to refer clients to trusted copyeditors and proofreaders
3. Other freelance editors who work exclusively with indie authors
4. Writing craft bloggers who need guest bloggers

PART 2

NETWORKING TACTICS

So far, we've defined *networking*, evaluated your current network, identified your most pressing networking goals, and considered whom to network with to support those goals. As we said at the beginning of this workbook, to network successfully, we must prepare to network. So now that we have the foundation down, let's turn to the tools and tactics we need to have in place to support and build our ideal network.

CHAPTER 5

NETWORKING TACTIC #1
A WEBSITE

A website will promote you 24/7: No employee will do that.

—Paul Cookson, marketing consultant

When someone is looking for an editor, one who does the work *you* specialize in, the first thing they're most likely to do is hop onto a browser and type in, for example, "mystery" and "editor." If you don't have a website, or you have one but lack the appropriate keywords, you won't be found. But if you have a strong, targeted online presence, your name should come up. Without that, someone else's name will pop up first, and there's a good chance your potential client will find the editor they've been looking for, or the information they needed, with the first search results. A professional website won't ensure that you're at the top of the Google results, but it's a critical first step in building an online presence that will support you in your networking efforts.

WEBSITE AS NETWORKING TOOL

When new editors ask us what they should focus on early in their careers, we first recommend continuing education—and then we suggest a website. Unless you're a veteran editor with a deep network that has consistently brought you more business than you can handle for years on end, you need a website.

Your website is the professional version of *you*, but on the internet. In old-school business terms, it's a storefront. But for freelance professionals, it has the potential to be so much more! Just as you would introduce yourself to a prospective client in person (stating who you are, what you do, telling them how you've helped other people like them—basically, laying the foundation for a business relationship), a website is one way we replicate that experience on the internet. It's a chance for anyone with internet access, anywhere in the world, to meet you and begin to develop a sense of who you are, what you're like, and how you can help them solve their immediate editing needs.

But how exactly does having a website serve your networking efforts? A website gives you a place (that you own) where you can do things like

- Share your knowledge via a blog or articles (thereby establishing your expert status and creating organic opportunities for interacting with visitors)

- Curate downloadable/printable resources for peers and potential clients (showing that you're knowledgeable, while helping others solve their own challenges)

- Establish credibility through testimonials

- Define your brand (from tone to niche to voice and visual brand markers)

- Set expectations (it's never too early to set expectations—or boundaries)

- Show that you're a real person, not a computer on an uninhabited island

- Share samples of your work (if you have the authors' permission)

- Explain your services in detail (positioning yourself within the publishing process, so visitors can tell at a glance if you might be able to help them)

- Provide quick guidance for people who are not serious about hiring an editor, or clients who are not an ideal match for you (in regard to editing niche, budget, etc.)

- Highlight your specialty or niche (if you have one)

- Communicate in your unique voice

There's overlap and interconnectedness in almost everything we do as freelancers, so it's no surprise that a website can be a networking tool, a marketing tool, a sales tool, and much more. That's why we're encouraging you to think about how your website can *specifically* support you as you *prepare to network*.

By having a website that tells your story and positions you within the editing community, delineating your skills, ideal clients/projects, and specialties, you'll be ready to benefit from all the other networking work you're already doing.

For example, let's say Renna, another of our editing colleagues, attends a conference and another editor, Jae, is impressed by her knowledge and professional attitude, so they want to add her to their referral list. As soon as they get back from the conference, they look her up online. She has an EFA profile, but no website. Or perhaps she has a website, but it's geared toward a very different genre from what she's currently specializing in (for example, Renna's website describes her as a developmental editor of children's lit, but she told Jae that her current focus is on proofreading noir thrillers).

This puts Jae in an awkward position. They believe that Renna would do a great job on whatever project she takes on, but they also know that it won't work to give her as a referral to a thriller author they can't fit in their schedule. The author will question both Renna's suitability for the project and Jae's judgment (or listening skills) for recommending her. This one disconnect—having a website that doesn't align with her goals (or having no website)—sabotages Renna's investment in the conference and potentially undermines her relationship with Jae. This is a made-up scenario, but it's based on our observations of "referrals gone awry."

This is why we view our websites as one of the first foundational tools in our approach to networking. Whether you're updating an existing site or creating a whole new website, you'll use the primary goals and building-block goals we identified earlier to shape your website's focus and message.

For example, revisiting our editing colleagues from chapter 3: Ana might add a curated resources page and monthly blog to help establish her reputation and build her brand. In her "About Me" section, Joy might highlight her in-house publishing experience and let visitors know that she's now offering freelance editing, which gives everyday indie authors access to a New York editor. Taylor might use their website to sell a digital toolkit, conduct an online technical editing course, or book speaking engagements. And Alex might host an "ask the editor" blog geared toward helping new editors entering his niche, which can help him build relationships with other editors who appreciate his expertise while also showing potential clients the depth of his knowledge in their specific subject matter.

Each of these activities helps the editor become known to both peers and potential clients, and each activity contributes to building the trust that's at the base of every relationship.

Seventy-five percent of users admit to making judgments about a company's credibility based on their website's design.

—STANFORD WEB CREDIBILITY RESEARCH

ASSESS OR CREATE YOUR WEBSITE

Assess

If you have a website already but are haunted by the sinking feeling (or outright evidence) that it's not representing you well, a first step is to do a quick online search with a few keywords that you feel fit your profile, and then notice which other editors' websites come up. (Warning, this is where impostor syndrome can creep in! The purpose of this exercise isn't to make you [or us—we've done this exercise too] feel "less than," but to gain a constructive perspective by visiting the sites of editors who offer similar services.)

Experience those sites first as a potential client. Take note of visceral reactions to the color scheme, the aesthetic, the fonts, the use of imagery, and the organization. Do you instantly trust this editor? Do you immediately question their professionalism? Are you filled with excitement or bored before you even start reading? Can you tie these emotional reactions to specific stylistic aspects of the website, regardless of the text?

Now experience the sites wearing your "freelance businessperson" hat. And remember to view these surface aspects of each website through the lens of networking. After all, if you're trying to build relationships with visitors to your site (whether peers or clients), your site's "vibe" is important. Quite often we make instant decisions based on instinct or unexamined evaluative processes. Pay attention to the sites that impressed you as professional, confidence inspiring, and interesting. From a visual standpoint, what do those sites have in common?

Now flip to your website. It's hard to be impartial, but try to separate yourself from the words (and the fact that it's your site) and just notice the same visual cues—color scheme, aesthetic, fonts, imagery, organization. What does your site have in common with the sites you liked (in your guise of "potential client")? What does it have in common with the sites that made you react with a "meh" or "no way!"? Take notes and maybe even print out screenshots of your landing page and the other sites' landing pages for comparison.

Next, list the pages (menu choices) that the sites have in common. How are the pages grouped? Is the flow logical to you as a potential client? Or does it feel more focused on the editor and less on your user experience?

Now go back to your site. Is it missing any pages that all the other websites have? Does it have a lot of additional menu choices? There isn't one right way to organize your website or a perfect number of pages, but there are best practices that provide a useful range for meeting most needs. (More on this in a bit.)

In this exercise, the goal is to 1) find websites of editors who share your expertise and niche, 2) evaluate how well their websites are working and note the observable aspects of their sites, and 3) use that information to reassess your own site. By taking notes and focusing on the quantifiable, objective aspects of the sites that inspire confidence and make you want to work with those editors, you can then apply those same techniques to your own site. Just remember, *never* copy or use someone else's content without their explicit permission. Creativity has no limits, so do your best to be *you* on your website. There are many people who can provide the same services you do, but your work will be a unique product of your style, experience, and approach. This is what sets you apart. So, make it easy on yourself and your potential clients by giving them the opportunity to get a sense of the person behind the editing service.

People assign more credibility to sites that show they have been recently updated or reviewed.

—STANFORD WEB CREDIBILITY RESEARCH

Self-Assessment Worksheet: Website

👤 Step 1: Your website

Website URL: _____

Editing services (examples: proofreading, line editing, ghostwriting, indexing):

_____

Genre/specialty (self-help, memoir, humanities textbooks, medical journals):

_____

Main site and font colors: _____

Main font styles: _____

_____

_____

_____

Images used: _____

_____

Page categories: _____

Professionalism: 1   2   3   4   5   6   7   8   9   10

Ease of navigation: _____

Call to action: _____

Ease of contact: 1   2   3   4   5   6   7   8   9   10

Editor-centric or client-centric approach? _____

Instant emotional reaction (from "I would work with this person" to "Meh" to "No way!")

1   2   3   4   5   6   7   8   9   10

Self-Assessment Worksheet: Website

👤 **Step 2: Websites for editors offering the same services in the same genre/ specialty (choose five and complete the following exercise for each)**

Website URL: _____

Editing services (examples: proofreading, line editing, ghostwriting, indexing):

_____

Genre/specialty (self-help, memoir, humanities textbooks, medical journals):

_____

Main site and font colors: _____

Main font styles: _____

_____

_____

_____

Images used: _____

_____

Page categories: _____

Professionalism: 1   2   3   4   5   6   7   8   9   10

Ease of navigation: _____

Call to action: _____

Ease of contact: 1   2   3   4   5   6   7   8   9   10

Editor-centric or client-centric approach? _____

Instant emotional reaction (from "I would work with this person" to "Meh" to "No way!")

    1   2   3   4   5   6   7   8   9   10

Self-Assessment Worksheet: Website

👤 Step 3: Compare and contrast

Which site do you like the most? The least? Why? _____

_____

_____

Which site is confidence inspiring? Why?

_____

_____

Which creates excitement about the prospect of working together? How?

_____

_____

What do the top two sites have in common? _____

_____

_____

What do the bottom two have in common? _____

_____

_____

How can you apply the lessons from the most engaging sites to the development or revision of your own site? _____

_____

_____

_____

_____

_____

_____

Create

Maybe you don't have a website at all. You've gotten by for years without one. To tell the truth, you've tried to create one a couple of times, but it just hasn't worked out. You're still getting projects, though, so—is it really necessary?

That depends. Are you content with the freelance career and professional support network you have today? Are you confident they will be there for you tomorrow too? If there's a chance you could be doing better—more satisfying work, better clients, making more money, or being part of a supportive editing community—then, yes. Let's build that website. It's not too hard. And it doesn't have to be expensive.

Creating a website isn't rocket science. Today many services will do everything for you for a minimal investment. With these services, you can create a basic and attractive website in one to two hours. If you don't have a website, and don't have the time to create one with the four basic pages ("Home," "Services," "Testimonials," "Contact Information"), then consider at least having a one-page website (for now): a simple landing page for your business that tells your clients you are real.

Some tech-savvy editors love the experience of building their own site. Some of us started building our website on our own, using WordPress and watching YouTube videos. We learned how to add plug-ins, use widgets, and organize our content. It's really up to you to decide what your comfort zone is (time, budget, and an interest in learning something new).

A mistake many of us make when we build our first website is that we build it according to what *we* like, without considering what our *audience* is looking for. Your website has to be well presented and dynamic (adapting to mobile views); it needs to have good keywords for search engine optimization (SEO). It should be informative and to the point, conveying exactly **who you are, what you do, and how to get in touch with you**.

Yes, creating a website from scratch is a project, but it's a reflection of you and your work. Once your website is up and running, the regular time commitment is minimal, though it will need to be updated at least once a year to make sure the information is still accurate *and* relevant. We all change, as do our businesses. We're dynamic human beings, and the media that represents us should also be dynamic.

Website Checklist

Whether you're creating a new website or using the takeaways from the previous self-assessment worksheet to revise your existing site, there is a checklist you can follow in appendix B (p. 137) to make sure you have a solid site.

For now, let's review what good information architecture for a website looks like:

- Landing page/home page

  o Place company name (or your name) front and center

  o Be sure to use your full business name

  o Include an up-to-date profile picture

  o Provide easy-to-find contact information and social media links, ensuring that they're visible and clickable (meaning if a person clicks on one, it will take them to that site, ideally opening to a new page)

  o Make sure the type of editing you do is front and center (don't make clients guess)

  o Check that all the information above exactly matches what you have on your social media networks/business card/directory profiles, etc. Remember, consistency is key to brand recognition!"

- Services page

  o Clearly state every service you offer and what each means or entails

  o Don't list services you *don't* offer, or services you have no experience with

  o Consider offering editing packages or customizable packages

  o If you list your rates, make sure they are up to date. If you don't want to list your rates, a good practice could be stating "My rates are updated every year. Please contact me for a quote or proposal," or "My rates are based on the Editorial Freelancers Association's rates chart," etc., with a clickable link to that page. If

---

** Note: If you don't freelance full-time, or if editing is a side job for you, it may be hard to have your social media or website match across all platforms. Just try to make sure it's as consistent as possible.

your rates are negotiable, state that as well. Clients want to know whether you can adapt your rates or offerings to meet their budget. (And if it's your policy to use a strict rate schedule, that's okay too. The idea here is to use your website to set client expectations.)

- Testimonials page
  - Include relevant testimonials from satisfied clients
    - List the name of the client with a link to their website/project/book page/ etc. Include a photo of the client, if the client agrees.
  - List best testimonials first, or newest to oldest
  - Make sure each testimonial reflects one of the services you offer

- Contact page
  - List your name, pronouns, and preferred contact method
  - If your email address is provided, make sure it's clickable
  - If you use a form that the client needs to fill out, make sure it's working (It's easy to test a contact form; remember to do so periodically.)

Once you've implemented these website basics and have designed your website as an effective networking tool, make sure to list it in your email signature line, on any online profile you keep with organizations or social media platforms, and on your business cards too. You want to be sure that the great client you're trying to land can easily find you and connect—and that colleagues who are trying to refer work to you can do so easily, without spending too much time looking for your information.

SEO

If there was ever an acronym that meant so much to freelancers these last few years, it's *SEO*. Search engine optimization is everything to a website. There is so much to say about SEO and how we can harness it for our websites that at times it feels like a rabbit hole we're afraid to enter, but know we need to if we want to be found online.

Because it's beyond the scope of this book, we won't go into detail about SEO, but we do recommend you inform yourself, learn about it, and maybe even take a class. For example, editor Michelle Lowery has years of valuable experience in this arena and offers an excellent class on SEO.

> *Search engine optimization is an ongoing process. There are always more keywords to optimize, more content to create, more links to get, more rankings to achieve, more traffic to build, and more conversions to fulfill. There is never a day when the SEO gets to sit back and say, "It's done!"*
>
> —STONEY DEGEYTER,
> *DIRECTOR OF DIGITAL MARKETING FOR* SEARCH ENGINE JOURNAL

INSIGHT: ACCESSIBILITY

Whether you're designing your website, tweeting a link to your latest blog post, or uploading a video to Instagram, take a moment to consider how to reach as many people as possible—while creating a space that *welcomes* as many people as possible. After all, social media is a tool for building community (and networking), and for it to be effective, we need to invite people in rather than shutting them out. We need to make sure that we're not perpetuating barriers that will keep anyone from the tools and support they need to accomplish their goals. A good way to do this is by learning about accessibility tools and practices. When we make these inclusive tools and mindset part of our default approach to networking, more people will be able to engage with us and our content—and our network will benefit.

Many platforms, such as Squarespace, Wix, Facebook, Instagram, YouTube, and Twitter, have built-in accessibility tools and user guides, and we've also included some starter resources in appendix E. Easy first steps include making your content more accessible to screen readers (assistive technology/software that helps blind and low-vision readers use digital content) by doing things like tagging photos and videos with alt text, providing captioning for audio resources/videos, and using camel case in hashtags (#NetworkingForFreelanceEditors rather than #networkingforfreelanceeditors).

In addition to improving accessibility, these minor adjustments also make your business communications more effective and useful to your audience. For example, using alt text has definite SEO benefits. These short, descriptive phrases allow search engines to access visual content that they would otherwise not have access to (for instance, the JPG of that cool lay/lie infographic you created). You can also link to a text-based version of informative visual graphics, which aids SEO and allows screen readers to access the actual content.

In addition, when you design images or decide on your brand colors, pay attention to color contrast and how it affects readability for people with color blindness. Likewise, some fonts are more accessible for readers with dyslexia. Be mindful of how your default choices might make it easier or harder for you to reach and connect with potential clients and colleagues online.

It may seem like there's a lot to learn if you want to make your content and communications accessible, but don't get so overwhelmed that you don't even try. Creating accessible content is within your power. Check out the resources in appendix E to get started.

Quarterly Networking Worksheet

Action for My Website:

Editor Check-In:

After completing the website self-assessment worksheet, Ana realized that her website screamed "fangirl," not "professional editor who can get your novel ready for prime time." Here are the top-level changes Ana decided to implement to get her website working for her as part of her networking strategy.

Action for My Website:
1. Tone down the neon color scheme; study mystery genre covers and adopt the colors and fonts of my dream clients' books
2. Rewrite content to focus on the client's needs
3. List professional memberships to build credibility
4. Curate blog content to be more targeted and helpful to indie mystery writers

CHAPTER 6

NETWORKING TACTIC #2
PERSONAL COMMUNICATIONS

It's up to you to create the opportunities for finding connections.

—MICHELLE TILLIS LEDERMAN, THE 11 LAWS OF LIKABILITY

It's easy to underestimate the impact that our daily personal communications have on our networking efforts. When we think about a networking plan, we tend to envision a radical commitment to a new way of putting ourselves out there. Something challenging, maybe a little scary—definitely outside our comfort zone. But a happy fact is that networking starts with something as small as how we interact with each person we come into contact with—and we have the power to build our network with something as simple as each email we send.

Were you expecting a herculean task? Is this too easy to be worthwhile? Keep in mind, it will take discipline and thoughtfulness—being aware and in the moment when you might prefer to just phone it in. Relationships are built bit by bit, and when we focus on our communications as an intentional networking tactic, we can leverage the power of incremental growth.

In this context, what counts as "communications"? Our focus will be on email because it's one of the activities most of us have to do every day, but other examples include social media posts, commenting on group platforms—even something as straightforward as an invoice or an out-of-office message. (Linda has the record for the best out-of-office message. Instead of a disappointing, bland notice that she was unavailable, her message featured an illustration of an idyllic beach scene and let Brittany know that she was busy recharging her batteries but would be back energized and better than ever on the following business day. Yes, it made Brittany wish for some beach time of her own, but it also made her happy for Linda and strangely refreshed just from that brief thought of enjoying a day on the sand.)

So, how do we make everyday emails work for us from a networking perspective? Admittedly, this is, in many respects, a less targeted networking tactic than crafting a website, but by paying attention to how we interact with others on a fundamental level, we can develop good communication habits that will make us more successful at cultivating relationships. Let's consider how the message and the medium of our personal communications can contribute to building the network we need.

THE MESSAGE

Networking gets results when we are real and do our best work—when we show that we are easy to work with, conscientious, and professional. We all have bad days, but in networking, we want to build up a picture of who we are on our best days: someone people want to hire, someone they want to recommend to their own clients (if we provide an adjacent service), someone they want to send overflow to. Someone they trust.

So, it's important to be mindful of how we present ourselves and where we focus our energy. We might not always have the wherewithal to be upbeat and personable at the end of a long day, but we'll take the extra five seconds to type out the name of the person we're communicating with—and to close with a "thank you"—rather than firing off a one-liner. There's another person on the receiving end, and they've had a long day too, so take the opportunity to connect with them, even if it's just acknowledging that they're more than just a dispenser of needed information.

Remember that part of building networking relationships is creating room for positive interaction. This means being approachable, showing that we're open to helping others when we can and are interested in their work and challenges. In the years since we first codirected the EFA Diversity Initiative's Welcome Program, we've regularly been approached by new (and established) editors who are looking for guidance or advice. At first it was hard to imagine that so many editors had heard of the Welcome Program, which only started in 2018, but then we realized that we both try to be accessible and empathetic through our choice of volunteer work and interactions with others, and that people we don't even know pick up on it. Like many of our peers, we know what it's like to desperately need a word of assurance or the kind of perspective that only comes with years of experience. And because other editors took the time to answer our questions when we were starting out or working through challenges, we make the effort to do the same.

Does this lead to new business? Sometimes it does. Sometimes it doesn't. But networking is about more than increasing the bottom line. It's about building connections that enrich the individual and the group. It's about being open to possibilities and the serendipity that awaits.

Our takeaway: be present, be yourself, and share your strengths.

Communication Tips

- ✉ Regularly check in on clients and colleagues (congratulate them on successes, wish them a happy birthday, share articles, share your blog post, ask about their project's progress, etc.). Remember to leverage the incremental strength of frequent communication.

- ✉ Don't wait for special occasions—text, tweet, or email them whenever they're on your mind.

- ✉ You can also set yourself reminders if you often get too caught up in your deadlines to be spontaneous.

- ✉ Don't reach out only when you need something. Everyone wants to be appreciated for who they are, not just what they can do for you.

- ✉ Consider creating a newsletter to give your readers a chance to know you better.

- ✉ Keep track of multicultural holidays so you can be mindful of colleagues' schedules and show respect for their time out of the office.

- ✉ Empty your voice mail box regularly. Make sure it's easy for people to communicate with you.

- ✉ Invest in stationery and stamps—send notes!

- ✉ Acknowledge kindnesses with thank-you gifts when appropriate.

Everyday Communications That Need to Align with Your Networking Efforts

- Your voice mail message (Let your personality come through; be professional but engaging.)

- Your profile in professional directories (Present a consistent message/brand.)

- Updates posted on your LinkedIn profile (or the headline you use on LinkedIn)

- Your headshot on a social media profile

- Your bio as a speaker, award recipient, or board appointee

- Your invoice (Remember to thank your clients; remind them that referrals are appreciated.)

- How you participate in a Twitter chat

- Your #StetWalk pics and text (hat tip to Tanya Gold, @EditorTanya)

- The contact page on your website (Let visitors know your business hours and whether you reply within twenty-four hours/one business day, or another time frame. Set expectations and honor them.)

How you present yourself in any of these "networking encounters" is as important as a VIP invitation, a solid handshake, or an engaging elevator pitch.

THE MEDIUM

We often wish that there were a how-to-exist-in-a-business-environment manual that everyone received at the start of their career. It would tell you things like "be prepared to take ownership of solutions you suggest" and "learn the art of workplace triage." And a whole chapter would be devoted to email best practices, from using executive summaries to the benefits of bullet points to asking direct questions and indicating next steps.

For now, here's a list of some things to keep in mind when crafting effective emails that will show you as the drama-free freelance editor that you are. We've found that implementing these steps contributes to establishing trust with peers and clients, which makes it more likely that we can effectively network with them.

- Create email templates that you can customize. By preparing a thoughtful, helpful response to common requests ahead of time, you'll have more time to focus on engaging with your reader (by adding a personal greeting) and you'll sound less harried, abrupt, or curt. This is also a good tool to prevent the last-minute misspellings that crop up when we're in a hurry.

- Make sure to create a vacation response if you're going away for a few days; it lets your client know your absence is planned and that you'll reach them when you return to your office.

- Create a well-thought-out signature line. Maybe add your social media links or organizations you belong to (which enhances credibility). Or add a quote—whether it's your tagline or your favorite literary one-liner.

- Keep your reader's needs in mind when crafting emails:
  - Use a proper greeting. Take time to acknowledge the person at the other end; balance to-the-point emails with a friendly, welcoming attitude.
  - Acknowledge and appreciate your reader's efforts or contributions to date.
  - State the purpose of the email. Keep it to the point and focus on the details that are necessary for decision-making.
  - Use bullet points or other formatting techniques to keep important information or questions from being lost in the main text.
  - Ask direct questions.
  - Recap your understanding of the situation or the next steps. Be clear about dates and deadlines. Setting expectations is key.
  - Offer to answer questions (or even talk on the phone).
  - Thank your reader.

> *It's natural to focus on what we need, but connecting with others means listening to what they're saying and recognizing how we can help them reach their goals too.*
>
> —BRITTANY DOWDLE

Self-Assessment Worksheet: Communication Habits

👤 General

What are your preferred communication methods (phone calls, text, email, etc.)?

_____

Does your preferred method align with your clients' and colleagues' preferences?

_____

If not, what adjustments can you make to increase your comfort level while accommodating their needs?

_____

_____

What communication habits of others do you find most frustrating (running counter to clear communication)?

_____

_____

Which of your own habits might hinder clear communication and relationship building?

_____

_____

👤 Email evaluation

Do you routinely include an addressee line ("Dear Ana," "Hi, Joy")? _____

Do you include a personal greeting? _____

How do you sign off?_____

    Do you invite further discussion or signal your availability to answer questions?

    _____

    Are your website and social media links included in your signature?   Yes   No

    Is a business tagline included in your signature?   Yes   No

    Are the main professional organizations you're a member of included in your signature?   Yes   No

Are your messages long and detailed?   Yes   No

Are they as short as humanly possible?   Yes   No

Do you use bullet points to highlight specific questions needing answers?   Yes   No

Describe the general tone of your communications in three words: _____

_____

Now, randomly select five emails from your Sent box (no more than a month old).

Do your answers in the previous section match up with what you find in the actual emails? _____

Note the differences and evaluate whether adjusting your communication style might avoid misunderstandings, improve efficiency, engage your reader, encourage finding solutions, or create space for getting to know others and allowing yourself to be known as a person behind the edits.

_____

_____

_____

_____

Select a few emails from two of your contacts whose emails are consistently clear, actionable—and personable.

Apply the email evaluation questions to their emails and note the answers.

What takeaways can you apply to your own communication style? _____

_____

_____

_____

_____

_____

LINDA'S PERSPECTIVE

My first communications with clients are usually by email or by direct messages on Instagram. After a few email exchanges where I learn more about my client's project, I'll search for them online (vetting them) on LinkedIn, Facebook, Instagram, or Pinterest. This usually gives me a good idea of what their personality is like. Then, to verify we are a good match, I do a free thirty-minute consultation/interview to hash out any last questions I may have for them and vice versa. If we're both on the same page, I send them a contract and our work begins. For authors or editors I coach, we will usually do a weekly one-hour video call. For authors whose work I'm just editing, I'll usually stick to email and call only if I have some major query that I feel needs to be communicated clearly and immediately. I use the phone a lot these days to avoid email miscommunications too; sometimes a quick phone call takes less time than typing up an email, and most clients appreciate that I reach out to them in a timely manner.

AN EDITOR'S PERSPECTIVE

Most of my networking is done via email groups—asking questions, and answering when I can . . . When I travel, I usually post notices in my groups to ask if anyone wants to meet up for lunch or coffee. I've made a few good connections that way.

—ÆLFWINE MISCHLER, MISCHLER EDITORIAL

BONUS!

Things That Make Networking Easier

- A short, to-the-point pitch

- Email templates (for praise, for introductions, for rejecting work, for referring work, for thank-yous, for sharing resources)

- Testimonials on website or printed material

- Business cards

- Clickable contact information on everything that represents you (email signature, contracts, proposals)

- Asking for referrals/reviews on your invoice

- Samples of your work

INSIGHT: THE IMPORTANCE OF BEING . . . YOURSELF

Because networking is often spoken of as this critical but elusive magical elixir that we must obtain in order to succeed, many of us let that pressure spill over into our networking efforts. We expect instant networking results and sometimes treat others like networking PEZ Dispensers. We feel the need to be "on" all the time, to turn everyday encounters into hard sales pitches, or to squeeze the life out of every opportunity even when we would make a much better impression—and lay the groundwork for a real relationship—if we just took a breath and respected others' boundaries. The result of this networking pressure is that we sometimes come across as being rather self-centered, even if that's not our intention.

At the same time, some of us feel the need to self-censor, to strip our communications of personality so that we can fit in as "professional." The result is that we're uncomfortable, and we end up sounding flat or fake. At the very least, we just blend into the background. It's something others pick up on almost subconsciously, and it's a surefire way to sabotage our networking efforts.

None of this should come as a surprise—when we're under pressure, it's a natural reaction to want to doggedly push forward or, conversely, to stay safe inside the time-honored lines. This competing sensation is the networking version of "fight, freeze, or flight."

Instead, try to settle in—into being yourself.

We each have our own voice, which comes through in our speech, writing, and expressive choices—from our brand colors to our preferred fonts. That unique voice is an essential part of our networking—it's our signature. When we allow ourselves to be *ourselves*, to embrace our quirks and idiosyncrasies while still being hardworking, skilled practitioners of our chosen vocations, that's when we become, as Louise Harnby says, "interesting" and "memorable." That's when we feel comfortable in our own skin, when we have confidence in our abilities, and when we can make the real connections that networks are built on. Superficial networks don't create nurturing communities and don't bring the leads and opportunities that we're looking for. To build deep, effective, multilayered networks, we have to be—as clichéd as it may sound—true to ourselves. And in doing so, we can create networks that are inclusive, supportive, and enriching.

A network doesn't just have to be who you meet at work, but rather anyone in your 360-degree purview.

—Samantha Nolan, Nolan Branding

BRITTANY'S PERSPECTIVE

Who counts as a networking contact? Everyone you know! Current/former clients, employers, coworkers, website visitors, friends/family/neighbors (in person and online), professional service providers (your accountant, your client's accounting staff, your dentist—everyone in your personal network). Oftentimes we tend to think that our future clients are "out there" and we have to somehow find them, but the advantage of treating your daily interpersonal activities as networking opportunities is that it helps bring the "out there" over here.

The people in your personal network already know you; they know that you go the extra mile in your carpool duty, that you help your neighbor by watering their plants when they're on vacation, that you do little things to make other people's lives just a bit easier and less stressful. They see your work ethic and know you're easy to deal with. These are the people who can wholeheartedly recommend you when they know someone who needs their résumé edited, their first graphic novel proofread, their travel memoir indexed. And you don't have to be salesy or self-promotional to put your personal communications to work. You just need to be yourself— and not hide your work.

So, when your dry cleaner asks about your week, instead of saying, "I was swamped at work. If I never see another dangling participle, I'll be a happy camper," you might say, "I just finished an edit on an awesome alternate history fantasy. It was a lot of work, but I'm so excited to see it published." How many of their customers have such an interesting job? "Alternate history fantasy" is going to stick in their mind. And when their dentist tells them about the novel she's struggling with, your dry cleaner will be the hero who can put her in touch with a great editor.

Quarterly Networking Worksheet

Action for My Personal Communications:

Editor Check-In:

After Ana reviewed her own email habits, she realized that in her attempt to sound professional, she was in robot-editor mode way too much—and it was keeping her relationships on a superficial level. Ana chose four simple steps to help position her personal communications for more effective networking.

Action for My Personal Communications:
1. Take the time to say hello and connect on a human-to-human level
2. Make sure to respond to emails within 24 hours
3. Say "thank you" more
4. Come up with an engaging tagline for my email signature

CHAPTER 7

NETWORKING TACTIC #3
SOCIAL MEDIA

Make your Network a source of Joy. Build one full of people who you enjoy spending time with and helping. Who care about your development and success and with who you're comfortable revealing your setbacks and seeking their counsel.

—MARIE KONDO AND SCOTT SONENSHEIN, JOY AT WORK

In today's overwhelming world, where media follows us everywhere and we're expected to be actively engaging with our clients, potential clients, and colleagues—all while performing on social media platforms, saying something interesting and useful—networking can seem especially stressful. How do we keep up with trends? With technology? Whom should we really connect with? Which is the right platform to post what kind of information? Do we need to be on all of them? Will our private lives be revealed? So many valid questions!

Most of us started off on social media as a way to stay in touch with friends and family who live far away. It's been years since social media has evolved from just that (and not always in a positive way), but today we know through some hard data that being on social media is another important way to find and discover new clients (among an extensive list of other benefits and perils).

Whatever your beliefs are about social media, we want to encourage you to think of it as a tool in your kit that can bring great rewards if used correctly and in a manner that works for *you*. If you're social media averse (and many editors are), you can go ahead and hop over to chapter 8 (p. 99) . . . or consider staying with us to explore whether there are some fun, low-stress ways to make social media part of your networking strategy.

Forbes Insights published a study titled "Business Meetings: The Case for Face-to-Face," which discussed the perceived value of in-person meetings and networking versus virtual activities. Though many people preferred in-person interactions, others reported some distinct advantages of virtual engagement:

- Saves time (92 percent)
- Saves money (88 percent)
- More flexibility in location and timing (76 percent)
- Allows the participant to multitask (64 percent)
- Increases productivity (55 percent)
- Ability to archive sessions (49 percent)
- Less peer pressure (16 percent)

Interesting way to look at our social media time, right?

So, let's assess your current social media presence with the following exercise.

Self-Assessment Worksheet: Social Media Checkup

Which platforms do you have an account with?

Which platforms do you use on a weekly basis?

On which platform do you regularly engage with others?

Which is your favorite platform?

Which is your least favorite?

How do these platforms align with the platforms your desired network members use most (revisit chapter 4, if needed)?

For each platform you're on, ask:

Are you successful?

How do you define that success (number of followers/meaningful engagements/job opportunities/feeling in the know/learning new things/forming relationships)?

Are you measuring your efforts and results—or just going by feel?

CHOOSING A PLATFORM

We don't have all the time in the world to be on social media, so it's crucial to choose one or two platforms that we can work with—and that we actually enjoy using. Yes, *enjoy*!

Even if you avoid social media, you undoubtedly know the major platforms that are out there, you know which ones you've tried (successfully or unsuccessfully), and you probably know which you should consider using—in terms of both your target audience and your own comfort level. If you're not sure, try the short quiz by Interact called "What Social Media Platform Is Best for You?" Though it's not a one-stop solution to choosing a platform, it will give you a pretty good idea of where you should start based on your goals and your target client demographics.

Before we continue, a word about "The Best Social Media Platform for Networking": Let's dispel the myth right now. There is no *best* social media platform for networking. They can all be great—or time-sucking nightmares—depending on how you use them. Every successful editor we know uses or swears by different social media platforms. There are the unwavering LinkedIn fans. The Twitter devotees. The editors who only follow Facebook editing groups. Or those who connect on Clubhouse. Some of us are loyal Instagrammers. And others stick to Pinterest. There is no universal rule for what works best. What matters is what comes naturally to you, what you are interested in or willing to devote a bit of time to, and ultimately, where you can connect with your desired network members. Don't let anyone convince you one is better than the others. You might find a fit and be successful right from the start, or like us, it may take testing different waters to discover which platform you enjoy the most.

With that in mind, using the insights from chapter 4 about whom you want to connect with, let's find out where your ideal clients and colleagues are spending time online. Start by asking your former or existing clients what social media they use. Ask fellow freelance editors which platform works best for their social media strategy. If you don't know any editors yet, check out the organizations we list in appendix D, or the Facebook editing groups, and find editors who share your specialty. Where do these potential networking contacts spend time online?

Talking with your network about their social media strategy may also open the door to a deeper discussion, allowing you to discover opportunities to help your colleagues and clients as well. But even if you're not ready to talk with peers and clients about their social media, you can easily research where they are online and evaluate their content and engagement. When you know where they're most active, you can use that information to guide your own social media strategy.

Next, to add another layer of depth to this research, consider lurking on editor and writer discussion lists, forums, and message boards. Search for keywords that reflect your area of expertise (e.g., "academic editing," "translator," "ghostwriter," "book designer," "writer," "dissertations," "indexer," etc.). You get the idea! Do that same type of keyword search on Google, LinkedIn, or Medium. Focus on the platforms you enjoy using to understand what's happening there regarding these industry-specific topics. Combine this with what you learned by talking with clients and peers, then complete either the form below or the social media–overlap diagram on page 82 (or both!) so that it's very clear where *you* need to be.

Let's see what you've discovered so far.

Which social media platforms are my desired network contacts using?

Clients: _____

_____

_____

_____

_____

_____

Peers: _____

_____

_____

_____

_____

_____

Which social media platform(s) is comfortable for me now? _____

_____

_____

_____

Where is the overlap? _____

_____

_____

_____

_____

_____

_____

_____

_____

The Social Media Overlap

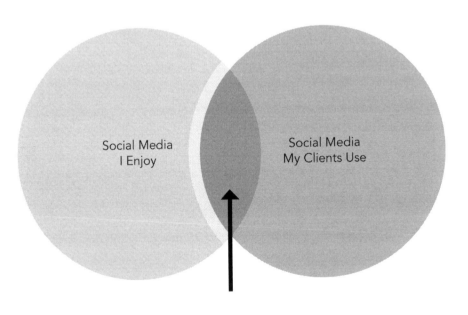

Social media–overlap diagram.

If there is overlap, then great! You know which platform(s) to focus your efforts on for this quarter. If not, then dig a bit deeper. Ask yourself, *Why is X social media comfortable for me?* Then ask, *How can I use this knowledge to help me succeed with the platform that my desired network is most active on?*

For example, our editing colleague Alex might be comfortable with using Facebook because he's been on it for years, but Twitter is overwhelming and chaotic to him. However, many of his target clients and fellow editorial professionals are most active on Twitter. How can he make Twitter feel more personal and focus his circle of engagement there? One answer is to use lists to craft a more custom Twitter experience. (Visit appendix C to learn more about creating a Twitter list.) By being open to examining his comfort zone and learning about his discomfort zone, Alex can create a compromise that will enable him to network more effectively with the people he most needs to reach.

This analysis of where your clients and peers are spending time online is something you should consider doing once a year—after you've set your business goals. This information is going to change over time, so what you write today will be different a few years from now, and that's how it should be. Some platforms will fall out of favor, and new ones will emerge. (This is one reason to make sure you have an online space you control: your website.)

Once you've worked through the preceding exercises and completed your research, you should have a solid idea of where your clients and peers are active online and which platform(s) you're willing to try. Now choose one to two platforms to focus and practice on for the next three months. We suggest a minimum of three months so that you have the chance to see tangible results and measure whether what you're doing is paying off. (How much time are you spending on social media? Are you forming relationships? Are you learning about your clients' needs? Are you building your brand?)

LINDA'S PERSPECTIVE

I love photography, gardening, baking, and home décor, so I'm naturally drawn to Instagram and Pinterest, which are more visual outlets for creative people. I like some blogs, but I don't have time to read many of them, so I follow very few bloggers, and usually, the blogs I do read are related to writing or editing. I spend very little time on Facebook, and when I do, it's only to post images of book releases or tips for writers and editors (even though there are some amazing editing groups I belong to and should participate in more). On Twitter, I follow a lot of agents and publishers to learn about publishing trends or what the market is looking for, but I don't feel I've fully grasped Twitter yet (probably because I have a tough time expressing myself in 280 characters!). So I lurk, occasionally comment when I have something of value to add, and take part in the occasional Twitter chat from the EFA. For now, I'm basically learning from others on this platform.

Since I do spend time on Instagram, I take advantage of what I've learned and enjoy, and I've created an account that's dedicated to book reviews, bookstagrams, and tips for writers (@lindaruggerieditor). A few years ago I took a self-paced class by Sara Tasker that I really enjoyed, which gave me some valuable pointers (Me & Orla). I've also studied the accounts I like and figured out what they have in common, and what I could build on my own page that reflects my brand, my style, my interests, and my work. Then, a lot of these posts get automatically shared on my Facebook author/ editor page, and on my Pinterest business account. I've slowly built a small yet organic following (without the help of outside agents), and although the number of followers may not be in the thousands, they are a tight, genuine, and curated group of creatives that I enjoy interacting with.

WHAT TO POST: CREATING MEANINGFUL CONTENT

Now that you've committed to trying a couple of social media platforms, it's time to decide what to post. As we mentioned earlier, if we're going to spend time (that it often feels like we don't have) on social media to attract clients and build relationships with fellow editors, we need to offer content that adds value. There are no set rules for editors for creating content; most of us discover our message as we go. The key, however, is that our content needs to bring value. We cannot stress that enough.

And remember, when you're on social media, you should always be doing one of these three things:

1.   Creating content
2.   Sharing content
3.   Commenting on content

If you maintain a balance between these three aspects of posting online, it ensures that you're contributing to your online community by sharing your own unique insights, curating and promoting quality information, and engaging with others.

Now let's return, for a moment, to our definition of *networking*: behavior that builds a web of mutually beneficial relationships. To get the most from our time on social media, we'll combine our definition of *networking* with our most important posting advice (add value). The result is a philosophy that helps us stay focused in the midst of social media information overload: build relationships by adding value.

As with all the networking tactics, using social media for networking comes down to using what you have (your unique voice and point of view) on the platforms you and your network like to use. The goal isn't to be famous or simply accrue ever more followers, but to reach your target audience (a.k.a. the potential clients who need you and your services, and the peers you can learn from and grow with). As you keep these guidelines in mind, your social media skills will improve and your network will expand to support your business.

Allow yourself to take the time to grow your audience *organically*. Let your followers come to you—as they discover you through your content.

And how do you do that?

By adding *value*.

By giving your peers and future clients information that will bring value to their professional lives. You might offer clients a tool, a word list, an idea, a hard-to-remember style rule, or an inspirational quote. You might share with other editors how you overcame freelancing challenges. The value you bring can be so many different things, but the starting place for knowing what to post is knowing whom you're trying to reach and what they need.

Get ready to brainstorm, and write your answers in the space provided.

For Clients

Who is my ideal client?

_____

_____

_____

_____

_____

_____

What do they need? (What problem can I help them solve?)

_____

_____

_____

_____

_____

_____

What content can I offer them, based on my expertise? (What solution do I have for their problem?)

_____

_____

_____

_____

_____

_____

As we discussed earlier, your fellow industry professionals should also be key players in your network. You'll learn from them, exchange ideas, help them and offer support, receive client referrals from them, and make client referrals to them when a project comes along that's not a good fit for you. Some of these peers you might already know, and some you have yet to meet.

For Peers

Who is my ideal colleague?

_____

_____

_____

_____

_____

_____

What do they need? (What problem can I help them solve? How can I support their work?)

_____

_____

_____

_____

_____

_____

What keywords do fellow editors use in their directory profiles and bios?

_____

_____

_____

_____

_____

_____

What topics do they discuss on social media?

_____

_____

_____

_____

_____

_____

How can I add to the conversation? (What kind of content/engagement can I contribute?)

_____

_____

_____

_____

_____

_____

INSIGHT: LINDA'S SOCIAL MEDIA STRATEGY

Example

Linda is a nonfiction editor specializing in memoir, so she creates content such as advice for memoir writers, inspirational quotes, and memoir best practices. Linda shares pictures of memoirs (books) or pictures of books about writing (with a comment on why she liked them and who should read them). If she's posting on Instagram, she makes sure to include relevant hashtags at the end of her post (like #LatinxEditor, #DevelopmentalEditor).

She also shares content on LinkedIn, like articles or information from other professionals that might be valuable to editors and writers (using the hashtags #WritingCommunity, #EditingCommunity, or #FreelanceEditor).

She follows (on Instagram and Twitter) the hashtags #Memoir and #MemoirWriter. When she sees posts with these hashtags, she'll look at the ones that interest her, and if she feels a user could be a potential client, she'll comment with useful information or say something nice.

Results

Linda usually gets contacted for memoir manuscript editing and writer coaching sessions. Her followers are creatives from twenty-five to sixty-five years old, from all over the world, and most are first-time writers who feel their manuscripts are ready for editing or who want to make sure they're on the right path with their work. Not everyone who sends her a direct message becomes a client, but that's okay, because, for Linda, being on Instagram is easy, fun, and a wonderful creative experience. And if the content she's creating can inspire or educate a fellow writer or editor, then that's a positive outcome.

By looking at the content Linda is creating, you can get a pretty good feel for her personality too. Keep in mind that when clients come to you because someone else referred them, they'll often decide to vet you by looking at what social media platforms you're active on and what you're posting. Do they share the same interests? Do they feel like they have a sense for who you are? It might just be that one quote/photo/tip that you post that makes someone feel you are the editor *for them*. Sometimes, it's the content that creates the credibility your client is looking for.

SOCIAL MEDIA IN ACTION

Maybe your clients could benefit from reading about tips for writing their graduate dissertation, or strengthening a character's story arc, or finding a literary agent or publisher. Maybe they need to know the "Five Must-Do Things for Blog Content Writing." We can't tell you what content you should publish, but we can tell you it has to be relevant to the type of client you're looking to attract. And like all things, it will take time to build an audience. Give yourself three to six months to experiment and see what results you get, and if you don't feel you're gaining traction, you can try something else.

And remember that any post or comment can be deleted at any time should you make a mistake or change your mind. Don't let the fear of being imperfect stop you from posting. You probably have an edibuddy who will look over your posts when you're just getting started—and you can do the same for them. This is part of being in a trusted network—and all the more reason for you to cultivate your own.

Once you've determined *what* type of content you can offer, it's time to envision *how* you can offer it—in a way that's easy to access and attractive. Using the keywords that identify the type of services you offer, search through your chosen platform and see what kinds of posts are appealing and pique your interest. This is not so you can copy what someone else is doing. It's to get you thinking about *what you like* and *what you can do*. The content you share should reflect your brand colors (maybe even the same font you use on your website), your voice, and your style. Make the content yours and be consistent so people can identify your brand!

When you look at how others are sharing their content, be analytical. Notice what content is original and what is shared or repurposed content. If you look closely, not everything you post has to be perfect or original. Sometimes sharing someone's post that you appreciate is enough.

To get you started, here are some of our favorite people to follow on social media.

Facebook

Louise Harnby; Training for Editors and Proofreaders group
Malini Devadas (editor coach); Edit Boost group

LinkedIn

Cynthia Williams (technical and business editor)
Crystal Shelley (fiction editor, authenticity reader)
Michelle Lowery (digital content editor)

Twitter

@bradmeltzer (Brad Meltzer, author and editor)

@thecreativepenn (Joanna Penn, author, creative, entrepreneur)

@sciEditor (Adrienne Montgomerie, sci and ed tech writer/editor)

@GramrgednAngel (Karen Conlin, the Dark Angel of Editing, fiction editor)

@FriendlyAshley (Ashley Bischoff, technical and business copyeditor)

@EditorTanya (Tanya Gold, book editor, writing coach, and translator)

@ArrantPedantry (Jonathon Owen, copyeditor and writer)

@mnbookgeek (Madeleine Vasaly, copyeditor and proofreader)

@wisekaren (Karen Wise, cookbook copyeditor)

@ZrAlexKapitan (Alex Kapitan, the Radical Copyeditor)

Instagram

@me_and_orla (Sara Tasker, UK Instagram expert, coach for creative businesses)

@5ftinf (Phillipa Stanton, artist)

@btleditorial (Hannah Bauman, editor, author, and writing coach)

@jningwong (Joan Wong, cover designer)

@heidifiedler (Heidi Fielder, children's book editor, writer, and instructor)

Pinterest

Aerogramme Writers' Studio (writing resource)

Jody Hedlund (best-selling author)

Silvia Day (*New York Times* best-selling author)

Pantone (company)

Thirty-five percent of survey participants said a casual conversation through LinkedIn Messaging led to a new opportunity.

—LinkedIn Corporate Communications

Other Ways to Gain Organic Followers

Another way of making yourself and your services known is by mindfully commenting on other people's posts. The key word here is *mindfully*. You don't want to come out and blatantly state that you're an editor they can hire for their dissertation or manuscript, or, worse yet, correct their grammar publicly. (Everyone despises the grammar police! UK editor Denise Cowle addresses this in her article "Why the Grammar Police Aren't Cool.") Instead, you want to think of how to encourage writers with their work and offer some insight, whether by suggesting a book to read or sharing a piece of wisdom that helped you overcome a writing challenge.

The behavior we're recommending to create organic growth looks like this:

The potential client you've found posts something about their manuscript.

You comment by encouraging them on their journey, or suggesting a solution to their problem.

Your potential client doesn't know who you are but appreciates the feedback, and likes your comment.

They check out your social media profile and follow you back. They get notifications when you post.

The next time they have a project, or know someone that needs editing, they reach out to you.

Blogging (or even writing mini blogs if you're tight on time) is another great way to drive organic social media growth. For example, if your platform of choice is LinkedIn, the options for networking are endless. Initially, most of us used this platform as a place to create our résumés and look for jobs. However, nowadays LinkedIn has become so much more than that, and if you use it wisely, you can reap a lot of benefits from it.

So, if you don't have a website or blog where you can post your ideas, do it on LinkedIn by creating a LinkedIn article, which is basically a blog post that's written right there on your LinkedIn home page (it's a small orange icon at the bottom right of the "Start a post" window).

If you'd like to create an article (for example, "Five Tips for Hiring the Right Mystery Editor"), make sure to include a background image, use keywords (to improve your SEO), and include at least one hyperlink (where the reader can find more information). Make your articles short, sweet, and meaningful. For information on how to do this effectively, you can check out "Publish Articles on LinkedIn." (More guidance on how and what to post on social media, as well as the link for this article, is located in appendix C.)

Remember, the key is to share information your target audience is interested in, while showing your personality and interests.

LINDA'S PERSPECTIVE

It's worthwhile to find ways to incorporate your social media networking into your everyday work. For example, I recently booked a Spanish proofreading cookbook project whose target market was Mexican readers, specifically. Knowing this, I reached out to an editor colleague in Mexico City and asked him where he thought I might run into trouble, just as a way of "opening my umbrella." We talked, and he referred me to a source I hadn't used before, the *Diccionario Panhispánico de Dudas* (*The Panhispanic Dictionary of Doubts*). (Interesting fact: Regarding whether a decimal number is set by using a point or a comma, it turns out that a comma should be used. However, this resource clarified that the comma is the preference in Spain and South America, but that in Mexico and Central America the point is preferred.) This was a perfect resource for the project I was about to undertake.

If I know the target audience, I might prepare by reading blog posts on editing for cookbooks, and maybe comment after each article with my own insight or questions. I'll research earlier cookbooks by this author to understand their writing style, or ask for a sample text from the publisher to get an idea of what the project is going to look like. After I'm done with my project, I may write a short article to share my own tips and advice for editing recipes by creating a post on LinkedIn or on my Facebook business page. If the experience was a positive one, I may reach out and connect to the person who hired me on LinkedIn too, or send them a thank-you email or card and ask that they keep me in mind for future projects. For sure, once the book is out I'll do a bookstagram (an artistically composed photo showcasing the book) of the cover on Instagram and a short post on my main social media channels stating what an honor it was to work on the project, with a link to the book sales page. These are all small networking activities that help me engage with my work, my colleagues, and my clients—and keep me out of my lone-freelancer box. (If you want to see an example of a bookstagram, head over to appendix C.)

SCHEDULE YOUR CONTENT

We find that we are most effective and efficient when we schedule our social media work in our calendars. Pick two or three days out of the week, and schedule what type of work you could do.

- Stick to simple, manageable tasks (e.g., "Monday: comment on five posts").

- Stick to attainable goals (e.g., "Wednesday: one original content post on LinkedIn").

- Find non-time-consuming posts (e.g., "Friday: share someone else's content with a short comment on FB").

- Make your social media accessible. Most social media apps have desktop versions that are easier to use (especially if you have to type!).

- Keep a folder with the content you post as a backup. Remember, you can repurpose that content again later in the year or next year.

- Consider using a social media scheduling platform like Hootsuite, Later, Buffer, TweetDeck, etc.

There is this rule that many people active on social media follow called the "30/30/30 rule." Although interpretations of it vary slightly, the one we feel helps us the most as freelance editors is by marketing strategist Paulette Duderstadt on LinkedIn:

30 percent of the time—be A LEADER in your industry on social. . . . Post about trends, business challenges and business outcomes, and information that is simply forward-thinking.

30 percent of the time—be A CHEERLEADER for your industry. . . . Too often [we] are laser-focused on posting all about the business. It's not all us, us, us in the business world.

30 percent of the time—be an ADVOCATE or AMBASSADOR for your community. Community means your employees, your clients, your neighborhood, and everything that you are passionate about. It may be raising awareness for an important fundraising event like a 10k walk that is aimed to do good.

So what happened to the other 10 percent? SHARE, SHARE, and SHARE. Sharing or liking or even commenting on social posts expands your reach and says that you are paying attention. So share what's important to your business and to you.

EXPANDING YOUR NETWORK

Here are a few more points for good networking etiquette while on social media. Check off the ones you are already doing:

- Follow people you look up to.

- Follow clients you enjoy working with (to learn about their business, their interests).

- Follow potential clients you'd like to work with (to learn about their business, their interests).

- Follow colleagues you respect (to learn about new business opportunities, classes, or trends).

- Comment mindfully and genuinely (avoid a standard comment that gets pasted everywhere, and avoid using only emoji unless you know the person personally and have that type of rapport).

- Don't follow people expecting them to follow you back.

- Don't follow people only to unfollow them later; in other words, don't follow someone just to get them to follow you back, and then unfollow them as soon as they do.

- Be mindful about commenting on controversial topics (politics, religion). It's important to be true to your convictions, but as a businessperson, be aware that the line between "personal" and "professional" is tenuous. Make sure you're prepared for the potential consequences of your words.

- Avoid social media if you are angry or upset, and never use it for venting about a client.

- Enjoy it and have fun!

AN EDITOR'S PERSPECTIVE

I once picked up a client through Twitter without even interacting with them on the site. A local in-house editor saw my feed, thought I seemed professional and knew my stuff, and passed my name on to her freelance manager, who emailed me.

—MADELEINE VASALY, MADELEINE VASALY EDITORIAL SERVICES

Quarterly Networking Worksheet

Action for My Social Media:

Editor Check-In:

Analyzing her social media presence revealed to Ana that she's been using LinkedIn a lot, which is great for connecting with other publishing professionals, but she's been avoiding Twitter, which is where a lot of indie authors are active. So, she's decided to get out of her comfort zone and research how other freelance editors are using Twitter, and then she'll create a plan that blends what she's learned with her current comfort zone. At the end of three months, she will have expanded her social media reach and—she hopes—her comfort zone.

Action for My Social Media:
1. Research colleagues who specialize in indie genre fiction and make note of which platforms they use—and how they engage with clients and each other
2. Test out the List function on Twitter and build a list of indie mystery authors to follow
3. Create a weekly plan for the two platforms I want to focus on

CHAPTER 8

NETWORKING TACTIC #4
PROFESSIONAL GROUPS

> *My top platform for ongoing networking is Facebook groups. They're free to use; can welcome editors 24/7 regardless of geographical location; can be broad or structured around a person or a topic; have a range of privacy settings to suit members' requirements, and provide a space for shy editors in which to lurk and learn without feeling uncomfortable.*
>
> —LOUISE HARNBY, FICTION EDITOR & PROOFREADER

Being part of a professional organization is an excellent way to stay informed of the trends, events, or news that could affect your business (both positively and negatively, like when AB 5 came out). Membership also provides access to vetted classes and continuing education opportunities. Some professional groups we encourage you to check out are ACES: The Society for Editing, the Editorial Freelancers Association (EFA), the Professional Editors Network (PEN), Editors Canada, and the Chartered Institute of Editing and Proofreading (CIEP). These are the groups we're most familiar with, but there are many other great organizations too. Appendix D has a more extensive list, and for an exhaustive list of editing- and publishing-related organizations, check out Katharine O'Moore-Klopf's Copyeditors' Knowledge Base.

Just remember—it's not about joining a bunch of groups (it will become overwhelming if you do). Instead, focus on the top one or two that resonate most with you now and promise the information and support that will move you closer to your goals. (As your career progresses, it's okay to drop memberships that are no longer relevant to the type of work you want to do. You can always go back to them later if you feel they would add value to your business.)

An effective way of determining which groups to join is to check in with your goals (the immediate and long-term ones) and use them as a guide to decide which groups might be a good fit.

If your goal is to gain new clients, ask:

- Which groups can help you reach and meet potential clients you can network with?

- Which groups have professional directories or job boards?

- Which groups market to potential clients on behalf of the membership?

- Which groups have conferences, live webinars, or meetups that will teach you something new, while providing opportunities to meet clients? (For example, the EFA often has a booth at the Writer's Digest Conference, so by joining the EFA you have access to its resources and the chance to represent the organization at client-facing events.)

- Which groups attend the specialty conferences that your target clients attend?

If your goal is to move into a new niche and you need to sharpen or acquire new editing skills, there are other questions to consider:

- Which groups offer educational webinars, classes, chapter meetings, or discussion lists?

- Which groups provide volunteer opportunities?

- Which groups support the trade publications in your niche?

- Which colleagues are in the know regarding industry trends, resources, and tools? What organizations do they belong to?

Once you've found an organization you're interested in, visit its "Resources" page.

- What type of information and resources does it offer its members?

- Does it have a membership directory where you can be listed? Can potential clients find you there?

- Does it have an online forum where members exchange ideas, tips, resources, and maybe even job referrals?

- Does it have a local chapter you can join (whether online or in person)?

- Does the website have an open job board or a job list?

- Does it have volunteer opportunities for members?

- What other membership benefits does it offer? (For example, does it have curated newsletters, discounts on software or insurance, free classes or publications, a mentorship program, or publishing opportunities?)

- How tech savvy is the organization? Does it have a professional, easy-to-navigate website?

- How much are the dues, and are there student rates or scholarships?

- Do current members encourage you to join—or recommend other organizations instead?

To help you decide which group(s) to join, use the following professional-organization comparison tool (you can download a free printable copy from www.networkingforeditors/resources). We've filled out the first line with an example to get you started. Because there are so many good groups, but we all have limited funds (and time), using a tool like this can help us evaluate which groups are most promising at this point in our careers.

 Before joining an organization, ask members about their experiences in the group; lurk a bit if possible before committing to an annual membership.

Self-Assessment Worksheet: Professional-Organization Comparison Tool

Organization	Location	Membership Cost	Targeted Toward	Has Educational Programs	Has Discussion List/Forum
Circle of Editors	US	$100	academic editors	yes	yes
Total Cost		$100			

Has Online Directory	Other Benefits	My Interest Level	Results	Renew
yes	mentorship program, discounts to spa resorts, coupons for loose-leaf tea	high	Was found by one client in first month. Received referral from fellow member that turned into work.	yes

If you join a group this year, but don't get a lot out of it (despite your up-front research), don't worry. That doesn't mean there's anything wrong with the group (or your research); it just means that either 1) it wasn't a great fit at this point in time (in which case, try another group), or 2) you joined the group, but didn't engage with its members. Networking is nothing without interaction. We can join groups and take in all the information on offer, but if we're not connecting with other humans, we're not maximizing the use of all that knowledge—and it may be harder to achieve our goals. So, reach out and participate, even if it's just to support someone else's comment, post, or idea—until you build the courage to post your own ideas, insights, and questions.

AN EDITOR'S PERSPECTIVE

Another key networking tool for me is industry associations. I belong to several, some for editors only and some for publishers and authors as well. I initially joined for professional development opportunities, but I soon found I enjoyed meeting people—a break from my solo practice. I'm often shy in big groups, but if I have a reason for being there, I can jump into conversations easily. So, if I'm at an association presentation, I can start conversations with strangers about the talk or the organization.

—**KELLIE M. HULTGREN**, KMH EDITING

INSIGHT: NETWORKING IN PERSON

This guide to networking was written during 2020 and 2021, so it's no surprise that much of our focus has been shaped by the need to find ways to stay connected while isolated. The editing conferences and smaller meetups we and our fellow editors enjoy have been on hold, and the plan forward is still taking shape. So, with an optimistic outlook, we wanted to offer some ideas for when we can all meet together in person once again.

Rethink Going National

While the national and international conferences get all the glory, they can also be challenging because of the cost of travel and lodging, not to mention the conference registration fee and time out of our work schedules. A few ways to make it more affordable include 1) volunteering to staff the registration check-in (some organizations give volunteers free or discounted admission), 2) sharing lodging (which is also a great way to have a guaranteed conference buddy), and 3) planning your vacation to follow the conference (for example, if you have to go to Denver for business, use it as a jumping-off point for sightseeing in the West).

Go Local

Check out local and regional conferences. The costs may be more feasible if you can drive instead of fly, and you might be able to reduce your lodging costs by having fewer nights away from home. From a networking perspective, another advantage of attending local meetings and conferences is that often they are smaller and provide the chance to get to know people better. If you don't love large gatherings, these small meetings can be less stressful and provide easier opportunities to socialize. And because these events tend to draw from the surrounding area, there's a good chance that you'll be able to keep up the in-person contact with the friends you make.

Be Kind to Yourself

Some of us are extroverted, and for some of us, it's an effort to feel at ease in an unfamiliar social setting. In either case, there are things we can do to get the most out of networking at conferences. One approach is self-care: pay attention to your nutrition, safeguard your sleep, and find ways to give yourself needed quiet time even in the face of the excitement and distractions of the conference. Another idea is to make plans to network and socialize while you're still at home in your comfort zone. That way, you won't feel pressure to make decisions on the fly, and you will have time to mentally prep for meeting lots of new people. For instance, before the conference, reach out to a few editors you know who will be there and arrange to meet for coffee at the hotel coffee shop between sessions, or get tickets for a local show, plan an impromptu photo shoot, arrange to sit with colleagues at specific panels, or plan a live tweet session to share the conference experience with editors who couldn't make it that year.

Be Prepared

Another part of the prep work that can make it easier to be comfortable with in-person conference networking is having business cards made well ahead of time and writing out conference notecards for yourself. What are conference notecards? Imagine having a small stack of 3 x 5 cards that you can flip through on the plane (or, in a list in the Notes section of your phone). On one card is your elevator pitch, on another is a list of three of your favorite projects, on another is a list of three of your most well-known projects. One card might have a getting-to-know-you series of questions to ask new connections, and another might have a list of current news topics in the industry. Nerdy, you say? Maybe so, but it's better to embrace your inner nerd than to draw a blank when the fifth person asks what your specialty is, or someone asks whether you've edited any authors they know.

Being prepared to network is a key part of our approach to networking. It allows you to make well-thought-out, mindful decisions that align with your goals before you ever venture out into the world. And it puts you in a position of confidence and ease so that you don't feel rushed, on the spot, or intimidated. That way, you'll be more comfortable being you—and that is what effective networking is about.

BRITTANY'S PERSPECTIVE

Since networking happens between individuals, it's good practice to approach each new contact as an individual. We all share identities with various intersecting groups, but we each deserve to be acknowledged on our own terms—to be accepted and valued—not erased or stereotyped.

Today, more people are recognizing the importance of accepting each other as they are—and showing that acceptance through welcoming, supportive behaviors. So when you venture into networking spaces, whether virtual or in person, keep in mind what you can do to put your budding relationships on a solid foundation. That might mean mentioning your pronouns, which can help normalize the practice and make spaces safer (but this should be optional—it's counterproductive to force people to self-identify). Or it might mean that before a call with someone whose name you don't know how to pronounce, you find out the correct pronunciation. For instance, I was recently preparing for a call with someone whose name was unfamiliar to me. A quick online search provided multiple examples of how to pronounce their name, including a recording of a talk they'd given that included a self-introduction. Finding out how to properly pronounce their name took me less than five minutes, but it allowed me to show respect and set the tone for our conversation. Being considerate toward others is one of the basic steps to productive networking.

Quarterly Networking Worksheet

Action for My Professional Organizations:

Editor Check-In:

Ana was a member of a few editing organizations when she first started out, but the dues were high and she felt lost in a big sea of veteran editors. Her professional-organization comparison tool showed that there are other affordable groups that are smaller and have a reputation for high-quality continuing education. And there are free options that are known for being supportive and welcoming of editors who specialize in genre fiction by indie authors. She's going to choose three groups to try out, and she'll reassess the situation in a year.

Action for My Professional Organizations:

1. Join Sisters in Crime and participate on a weekly basis
2. Join PEN and attend five webinars on topics that will help grow my business
3. Join the Editors Lair and connect with other indie specialist editors

CHAPTER 9

NETWORKING TACTIC #5
VOLUNTEERING

> *If you have helped an individual, and in some cases generally provided insight to others observing—helping someone learn something and feel more positive about freelance editing in general—then I think you've done successful networking.*
>
> —CRYSTAL WATANABE, PIKKO'S HOUSE

Have you ever noticed how people come alive when they're working on something they're passionate about? In the best cases, when people volunteer, insecurities drop away, the ego takes a back seat, and everyone is united by a common goal. No one *has* to be there, but everyone present *wants* to be there. Each person has something to contribute and looks forward to giving of their time, energy, and talents to accomplish some good—something that will benefit others.

That's the starting place for volunteering—the desire to give your best to help a like-minded group achieve goals that will benefit the community. Most people volunteer because they believe in a community or a specific goal, and they want to contribute. And in any volunteer work you do, that initial kernel of a giving spirit is critical. It's what puts you on the path.

But as we've discovered, volunteering, particularly in professional groups, is also a networking supercharger. No matter where you are in your career—from a newbie to a veteran—you can volunteer. And in doing so, you can expand and strengthen your network.

Volunteering can

- give you an inside perspective of your professional community (if it's a group like ACES or PEN) or of your ideal client's community (if it's a group like Sisters in Crime and you edit mysteries);

- give you the opportunity to meet others who are on the same career path but at different points in their journeys, which can be enlightening for both the newbie and the veteran;

- help you build your brand and become known among potential clients and those who might refer work to you;

- make you an expert (even if it's in one little corner of your professional world);

- help you discover colleagues who could be part of your small, trusted network;

- keep you up to date on the current issues facing your professional niche—and give you the chance to become part of the solution;

- increase the likelihood of your being top of mind when someone needs to give a client a referral in your specialty;

- increase your confidence and sense of satisfaction; and

- allow you to get out of your comfort zone and learn something new.

OPPORTUNITIES ARE EVERYWHERE

If you join a professional group that feels like "your people," one where you feel welcome, encouraged, and supported, at some point you'll find an opportunity to volunteer. Your first instinct might be to jump in. *This is so important to our group*, you think. *This is a chance to help others* . . . But then the part of yourself that's in charge of the calendar steps in. *Wait a minute, we don't have time for this!* And so the debate begins.

While *not* overcommitting is important (more on that in the next section), you might find it helpful to frame volunteer work as a chance to both give good and get good.

In other words, volunteering can be personally satisfying *and* amplify your networking efforts at the same time. It can bring a sense of community that's often missing in the remote working environment many of us are accustomed to, allowing you to build lateral relationships and learn from others in a low-pressure atmosphere. Quite often, specialized skills aren't required for volunteering; what's most important to volunteer coordinators is to have reliable people who do solid work and don't create drama. So, volunteering is an especially valuable opportunity for early-career professionals who are still trying to find their place and might not have the confidence that comes with experience.

One caveat in all this is that even though you're not getting paid for your volunteer work, for the networking-supercharger properties to be effective, you need to do your best work (within the time constraints, etc.). Remember, your main purpose is to help the group accomplish its goals. Dot the i's and cross the t's. Be the person who gets stuff done—and done right. It's not that you have to do *all* the things (burnout is real); it's that you want to honor your commitments.

And in doing so, you'll be building your brand—making a name for yourself as that indexer who's dependable and gets details right . . . as that academic editor who's the queen of follow-up . . . as that SF/horror developmental editor who keeps the Zoom meeting from continually spiraling out of control. And when it comes time to refer clients, share opportunities, or invite a presenter to the next conference, you just might be at the top of the list.

Because we don't live on an island—and no editor *is* an island—we all have interests outside of the freelance editing world. Think outside the box and tap into the other areas of life you enjoy. What are your hobbies? Is there a local group you belong to that could use your help and expertise? Maybe there's an opportunity at the animal shelter, or a knitting group, or a motorcycle enthusiast association. Have you tried connecting with a local food pantry or women's shelter? How about a community nonprofit? Or an advocacy group? The opportunities and organizations are endless—and usually within reach.

BRITTANY'S PERSPECTIVE

In my own experience, volunteering has essentially built the foundation of my network. I've been an EFA member since 2011, and I've staffed the EFA table at various conferences, but in 2016 I volunteered to work an EFA booth at a conference in San Diego. It was there that I met Sangeeta Mehta, who at that time was a newly elected member at large. We immediately took a liking to one another, and as we worked together over the course of three days, we discovered a shared interest in diversity and inclusion. Sangeeta mentioned that she thought it would be helpful if the EFA had an internal program to support these ideas, and I told her that if she wanted to pursue that back at the EFA headquarters in New York, she would have my support. Within six months, the EFA's Diversity Initiative (DI) was born. (I should mention here that Sangeeta is a powerhouse. I had an inkling of it when I first met her, but as I've worked with her in the Diversity Initiative for the last several years, I can say that she is one of the most selfless, determined, and giving people I know—and she has the ability to inspire those around her to work hard and pull together.)

Once the DI was up and running, and I began volunteering for various projects, I discovered that the EFA members who gravitated to the group were dynamic, diverse editorial professionals who shared my outlook and enthusiasm for creating a professional community where all are welcome and valued. It was here that my network grew and took root.

One of the early DI endeavors I helped with was the Welcome Program, which we envisioned as a welcoming space that would help new EFA members find their way in the group, build connections between members, and contribute to building a culture that valued diversity and inclusion within the wider EFA. After two years of internal development—with a significant investment of time by Sangeeta, Alissa McGowan (the first director of the Welcome Program in beta), and Kellie Hultgren—we were ready for the first full, public session of the Welcome Program.

By that time, I had met Linda through the Diversity Initiative. After one of our virtual meetings, she'd reached out to me via LinkedIn, and in doing so she noticed that we lived about thirty-five miles apart at the time. It took a matter of minutes to plan to meet for coffee and chocolate croissants, and the rest, as they say, is history. When Sangeeta asked me to lead the Welcome Program, I knew that Linda would be the perfect partner, and she graciously accepted. From there, we've gone on to form a mastermind group, present an EFA webinar, write this book, and generally support and cheer each other on. And Linda is only one of the supportive peers I've met through my volunteer work.

For me, volunteering has truly been a networking superconductor.

Self-Assessment Worksheet: Volunteering

👤 **Previous volunteer experience**

Pros: _____

Cons: _____

👤 **Your main goal and building-block goals**

1. _____

2. _____

3. _____

👤 **Issues that matter to you personally**

1. _____

2. _____

3. _____

👤 **Your top skills**

1. _____

2. _____

3. _____

👤 **Possible groups and activities to volunteer with**

1. _____   6. _____

2. _____   7. _____

3. _____   8. _____

4. _____   9. _____

5. _____   10. _____

👤 **List three to five opportunities that further at least one business goal, one issue you care about, and one of your top skills. (Choose one and commit to it for six months to one year, then reassess.)**

1. _____   4. _____

2. _____   5. _____

3. _____

EVALUATING YOUR VOLUNTEER WORK

In an ideal world, we could spend all our time working for the causes we believe in, and our best efforts would always pay off. But the reality is that most of us have to balance paid work with volunteer endeavors, and even when we do our best, the results don't always match our hopes, which can lead to burnout.

We've both been there, as have many of the people we've volunteered with. When you believe in a cause, it's hard to say no. Especially if that "no" might mean that an important program is put on hold or that planned resources take longer to produce. At some point, you may feel like if you don't do it, it won't get done. While these are challenges that all volunteer groups have to contend with, it's important to start with yourself and identify what's within your power.

So, here are a few things you can do to evaluate your volunteer activities and avoid volunteer burnout:

- Decide up front how much time you can commit to volunteer work (on a daily, weekly, monthly, quarterly basis) and stick to it. Don't overcommit!

- Be strategic and targeted. If you're volunteering for your local rabbit rescue, you don't have to be as strategic about it. Bunnies are bunnies. But if you're volunteering with professional or client-facing organizations, and it's part of your professional networking, then be strategic about which groups you volunteer with and which kinds of projects you take on. For instance, Brittany works with SF/F, historical fiction, and mystery, so she's not going to commit all her volunteer hours to the Board of Editors in the Life Sciences (BELS). 1) That's not where her passion is, and 2) that's not where her people are.

- Don't take on emotional responsibility beyond your role. As a volunteer, you commit to specific tasks and time commitments. Be clear about what you can do, and let the group adjust its goals based on its volunteer resources.

AN EDITOR'S PERSPECTIVE

I also try to volunteer my time with the organizations I join, and the people I've served with on committees and projects think of me when they need a freelancer. Just remember that many of these organizations are volunteer run, and they're always in need of more time and more energy. You can't fill every need! Volunteering means reducing the number of hours you have available for paid work, so establish expectations and hold firm to your boundaries when necessary.

—**KELLIE M. HULTGREN**, KMH EDITING

INSIGHT: NETWORKING INCLUSIVELY

Because the best networking is built on relationships, community, and being free to be your true self, it's critical to find and create networking spaces that are safe for all community members.

As we've learned throughout this workbook, we each have our own networking style—the place where our comfort level, natural communication style, and external engagement efforts align. For some of us, that's on social media platforms like Twitter and Facebook—for others, it's in one-on-one meetups or at conferences. While it's good to challenge yourself, it's also valuable to know what works for you and network in places (virtual and in person) where you feel comfortable.

Sometimes, though, it takes work to create those places—both for yourself and for others. And an environment that feels safe and welcoming to one person may be inimical to another person. Sometimes this comes down to personality (of the group and the individual), and sometimes it comes down to culture and identity—and how accepting people are of each other. Is the group welcoming and inclusive or off-putting and implicitly exclusionary?

Obviously, it's a complicated issue—and not one that can be fully addressed within the scope of this book—but it's important enough that we need to acknowledge that networking is influenced by cultural factors (see resources in appendix E for more about this). A space that feels safe for one of us might be inhospitable for another. Regardless of where you fall in the interconnected web of human identity, it's important to take care *of yourself* and take care *for others*. This awareness is a necessary part of building a vibrant network.

To that end, here are a few thoughts:

- Before joining a group, talk to its members. Find out whether it's welcoming and inclusive, whether it has issues with member retention, or whether there are subgroups within the main organization that are explicitly supportive (like a new-member subgroup or the EFA's Diversity Initiative).

- Look at the group's website or "About" page and read the subtext. What's important to you? Is it important to them?

- Search out groups that are a good fit for you, and consider building/joining a microcommunity within a group that has potential but is not there yet.

- Ask your trusted network which groups and platforms they belong to. What have their experiences been?

- Develop direct relationships with people who are also in a group you want to join; that way, even if you're a newbie, you're a newbie with friends and a built-in support network.

- If you're able to, speak up when you witness bullying or aggressive language. This might mean alerting a moderator, reaching out to the person being attacked, or calling out the bullying directly. Be safe and do what's within your ability.

- Listen to your own instincts. Your perceptions are valid.

- Keep searching. Be willing to create the place you seek, even if it's on a small scale, like a private mastermind group.

- If you're not sure how to support others, ask them. Then listen.

BRITTANY'S PERSPECTIVE

My level of involvement in editing discussion lists and in Facebook editing groups has shifted over the past ten years, as I've discovered my own networking style—and my own strengths and weaknesses. While I love the depth of knowledge, the encouragement, and the collective wisdom that can be found in these groups, after witnessing many episodes of unprofessional and damaging behavior, I started limiting the amount of time I spent in these spaces, and I invested my time in more person-to-person networking through volunteering.

That's one example of adapting to your surroundings and shifting your networking activities to suit your personal style.

Another example can be found in the story of the Editors Lair, an online editing forum created by Crystal Watanabe, the owner and lead editor of Pikko's House, an independent editorial business providing services to fiction and creative nonfiction authors. I've known Crystal (virtually) for several years—through Facebook editing groups, the EFA's discussion list, and the EFA's Diversity Initiative. I've admired her professionalism, her initiative, and her willingness to speak up—fairly but firmly. So when I received an invitation to join the Editors Lair, there was no question. Because I knew Crystal, I knew it would be an inclusive and welcoming place. As she explained to me recently, she created the Editors Lair because feeling alone was one of the worst parts of her first couple of years of freelancing, and she's never forgotten that. In creating this space, she wanted to provide a place for others so they wouldn't have to navigate this career path all alone. Networking wasn't on her mind when she founded the Lair, but that kind of community building is at the core of true networking.

Quarterly Networking Worksheet

Action for My Volunteer Activities:

Editor Check-In:

Ana is early in her editing career, but she knows that she already has experience and valuable skills to offer, so she decides to volunteer with groups that can give her the opportunity to get to know her ideal clients (indie mystery writers) and her fellow editing colleagues.

Action for My Volunteer Activities:
1. Volunteer with Sisters in Crime newsletter
2. Volunteer to staff the EFA table at Bouchercon
3. Volunteer with PEN's Mentorship Program

CHAPTER 10

PERSONAL NETWORKING STYLE

> *If we create networks with the sole intention of getting something, we won't succeed. We can't pursue the benefits of networks, the benefits ensue from investments in meaningful activities and relationships.*
>
> —ADAM GRANT, AUTHOR AND ORGANIZATIONAL PSYCHOLOGIST, WHARTON SCHOOL OF BUSINESS

In part 1 we looked at setting goals and identifying potential network members in order to reach those goals. Then in part 2 we reviewed the five networking tactics that you can use to build relationships with the people you need to connect with. For each tactic, you brainstormed steps to take and added them to your quarterly networking worksheet. Based on what you've discovered, it might make sense to say: my goals *plus* the people I need to reach *equals* the networking tactics I need to use. However, we would suggest that formula is missing a critical element.

MY GOALS

+ THE PEOPLE I NEED TO REACH

THE NETWORKING TACTICS I NEED TO USE

While it's important to have specific networking goals and plans in place, you also need to consider your natural communication preferences so that you'll *do the plan* and *reach your goals*. This is especially true for introverts. As networking expert Devora Zack explains, "Everybody is more than fine as they are. When we tap rather than cap our true nature, the sky is the limit." What does this mean? It means we don't have to change who we are; we are enough just the way we are. The secret, then, is recognizing and acknowledging to ourselves what type of networking we are comfortable with, and what type of networking we would not enjoy.

So the real formula is: my goals *plus* the people I need to reach *plus* my networking style *equals* the networking tactics I need to use.

MY GOALS

+ THE PEOPLE I NEED TO REACH

+ MY NETWORKING STYLE

THE NETWORKING TACTICS I NEED TO USE

Before working on the following self-assessment, look at your current network snapshot in chapter 2 to see where you've been networking up to this point. What you find there might indicate your baseline networking comfort zone.

Self-Assessment Worksheet: Personal Networking Style

👤 **What are your *preferred* ways to network?** _____

_____

👤 **Where do you feel most comfortable?**

In-person socializing (conferences, chapter meetings, literary festivals)?

Video and phone (webinars, virtual groups, mastermind groups)?

Email?

Online discussion lists and forums?

Social media: LinkedIn, Facebook, Twitter, Pinterest?

👤 **What new way of networking would you like to try?**

_____

👤 **What type of networking is of no interest to you? (This doesn't mean no forever, just no for now.)**

_____

_____

👤 **If you dread the idea of networking, what specific activities are you thinking of?**

_____

_____

👤 **Describe a networking plan that focuses on your preferred networking activities and is light on the ones you don't like doing.**

_____

_____

_____

AN EDITOR'S PERSPECTIVE

[I spend] some time each workday speaking up on Twitter, Facebook, and LinkedIn. I share news about the publishing industry and articles on how to run an editing business, appreciative notes from clients, news about my clients' publishing successes, news about helpful training and software, articles about good author-editor relationships. . . . I'm showing how skilled and knowledgeable I am and how wonderful I am to work with.

—KATHARINE O'MOORE-KLOPF, KOK EDIT

EXPLORING YOUR STYLE

Acknowledging and leveraging your personal networking style is the secret ingredient to making a networking plan that will work for you. Networking—putting yourself out there, meeting new people—it's all challenging enough without having to fight against your natural tendencies. So, work with what you have—and who you are right now. Maybe you just don't get Twitter, and if you have to become a Twitter pro, your networking plan is doomed before it even starts. But LinkedIn is your zone—you've gained three clients through LinkedIn and helped four colleagues connect with awesome opportunities. In that case, use your expertise and get creative. Make the most of your strengths. And maybe in a year you'll decide that you're ready to learn to tweet with the best of them: Who knows? That great connection you made on LinkedIn may need help getting their LI game up to speed, but they're a natural on Twitter. Help each other out! Teach each other how to make these platforms work for your needs.

Or maybe you don't like getting dressed up and going to conferences. Perhaps you find travel exhausting or you need to stay home to help care for a family member. Today, none of that has to limit your ability to make connections and build your network. You can sign up for virtual conferences, attend video meetings, or reach colleagues on the other side of the world—all without leaving your home.

There's no one right way to network. Do what you're comfortable with today, and respect what makes you "you." When you start in your comfort zone and make the most of it, you'll develop the confidence to exceed it—if you wish to (or, you may find you're exactly where you need to be).

FINDING BALANCE

Now is the time to take your completed quarterly networking worksheet and place it beside the personal-networking-style self-assessment. Your answers to this chapter's self-assessment worksheet will help you establish which networking tactics to pursue.

Do the networking tactics you've sketched out in the quarterly plan align with your personal comfort and productivity zones? Highlight the networking actions that might be a challenge for you based on your personal style. (You might think of these as residing in your "growth zone," a place of challenge and possibility.) Notice that we're not suggesting you cross the growth-zone actions off your list. We're just asking you to highlight them so you're aware of where your internal resistance might rear its head. If you've done the exercises throughout the workbook and put in the time and thought to craft a good plan, then believe in the plan.

BRITTANY'S PERSPECTIVE

I enjoy Pinterest and Instagram, but Twitter doesn't yet feel like a natural space for me. I used to be more involved in some of the great Facebook editing groups, but it's easy for me to get sucked into a social media time warp and emerge drained and flooded with too many ideas. Cue the overwhelming anxiety. I've found that the best way to manage that is to simply pull back from social media engagement, which has always been a bit of a stressor for me. The result is that I have a sporadic presence on a variety of platforms, which isn't super helpful.

But I know that social media has a potential place within my networking endeavors, and it comes down to figuring out how to make it work for me. Right now, I'm evaluating where I want to be active on social media, what my brand expression will be, whom I want to focus on reaching, and how to manage my social media in a sustainable, consistent way.

I've discovered that my networking comfort zone is nurturing one-on-one relationships with people I get to know through volunteering or shared interests. That's what comes naturally to me, and it's how I've grown my network—by making personal connections (usually over email, over the phone, or in person). My challenge here is to do the same through a medium that doesn't come naturally to me.

Editor Check-In:

As Ana worked through the answers to the personal-networking-style self-assessment, she realized that she enjoys interacting on Facebook and Instagram, but she has difficulty finding a balanced tone in emails. Ana also recognized that virtual spaces are much more comfortable for her than the prospect of attending meetings or conferences in person. Because of the pandemic, she's had the opportunity to attend many events virtually, but she feels that to move her career forward, she needs to be more comfortable with in-person gatherings.

As she reviews her completed quarterly networking worksheet, she uses this knowledge of her networking style to guide her efforts and shape her networking strategy for the next quarter. Because she knows that she'll be testing this plan for the next three months, after which she'll assess her progress, Ana has the freedom to experiment and be intentional about networking with purpose.

When we look at Ana's plan on the next pages, we see she has managed to include three of the five networking tactics: website (blog post), social media (Facebook and Instagram), and professional groups (PEN and Sisters in Crime). She's also going to attend a low-stress in-person event at her local library to acclimate herself to in-person networking. During each of these networking activities, Ana will keep in mind how they will help her achieve her goals of working with indie mystery authors, establishing her reputation as a freelance copyeditor and proofreader, and building her unique brand. The actual planned networking she does each week will shift according to her available time and the opportunities she finds to contribute to her network's growth and success, but her daily mindset—being giving, adding value, and connecting with others—remains active and constant.

This is what Ana's spreadsheet might look like for week 1 of her first quarter:

WEEK 1	Activity	Time Allocated	Whom Am I Reaching?
Monday	Join PEN and craft a directory profile that reflects my focus on mystery and related genres.	2 hours	Fellow editors in PEN, potential clients who search the directory for an editor to hire.
Tuesday	Start a short blog post (1,000 words) titled "How to Make Setting a Character in Your Mystery." Talk about this on Instagram and Facebook; ask followers for their favorite mystery settings.	1 hour	Mystery writers, past clients, fellow editors, potential clients, writers and readers of mystery fiction.
Wednesday	Search for indie authors who specialize in mystery, then choose five. Follow them on social media, look over their books, and check out their websites. Comment on one mystery-related post for each of them.	1 hour	Indie authors, other editors, novice writers who are fans of these indie brands.
Thursday	Join Sisters in Crime, explore the member area, and search for the closest local chapter (or an online chapter).	30 minutes	Mystery authors and editors.
Friday	Finish blog post. Have it proofread by a colleague. Post on my website. Share it on social media (Facebook and Instagram). Attend a mystery author chat at a local library.	1.5 to 3 hours	Mystery writers and editors, readers, aspiring writers.

NETWORKING TOP-PRIORITY TOOLS

My Website

Create, review, update, and personalize my website

My LinkedIn Profile

Create, review, update, and personalize my profile

My Directory Profiles

Create, review, update, and personalize my profiles

CHAPTER 11

AVOIDING NETWORKING PITFALLS

The obvious is only obvious when it happens to someone else.

—ANTHONY MARRA, THE TSAR OF LOVE AND TECHNO

Over the years, as active members in editing communities, in the US and abroad, we have tried to put our best efforts forward when meeting with clients, colleagues, and professionals who work in the publishing industry. We've attended conferences, volunteered for local chapters, hosted the Welcome Program for the EFA, taken classes, participated in webinars and panels, and written blog posts. We've hired colleagues, referred colleagues, and been the recipients of referrals. In each situation, we've tried to engage mindfully with everyone who crossed our paths.

But we know there are times we've missed the mark, when our best efforts at the time weren't good enough. With all the positives that have come from our careers as editors, we've also observed a lot of behaviors that were less than appealing, and inadvertently, we've surely been guilty of some of the same. While it's easy to pick up on these behaviors in someone else, it can be tough to recognize them in ourselves. Networking turnoffs we've experienced include bad attitudes, negativity, a lack of commitment, subpar work, blatant selfishness, the absence of empathy, and a focus on "networking-as-transaction." When listed like that, it's obvious that these behaviors will sabotage all our good networking efforts.

So, as only a true friend would celebrate our success, lift us up when we're down, and gently point out areas or conduct we might consider revising because it can hurt us, we've come up with six keys to avoiding pitfalls when networking.

BE PROFESSIONAL

Professional should be your default setting (which you can later relax as you get to know people). Being professional signifies different things to different people—whether in different countries or across cultures within the same country. To some, being professional is just a matter of knowing their stuff (a specialized knowledge). For others, it's not only about the knowledge acquired through schooling and experience, but a combination of education and everyday behavior. You can't control how another person will interpret your behavior, but you can be diligent about the business persona you project and about how you react in tough situations.

We've met editors who are very knowledgeable, and financially successful, but who lack professionalism when it comes to working with clients or colleagues. What do we mean by that? Well, sometimes editors can be rude or curt. Other times they don't deliver on what they promised or are too embarrassed to admit they made a mistake and don't own up to it. Some editors will share too much personal information with people they barely know, making a colleague or client feel uncomfortable. And sometimes a lack of professionalism has nothing to do with our skills and knowledge, but someone catches us at the wrong time, when our mind is engaged somewhere else and we can't answer that question, so we give a short answer, and all of a sudden we're labeled the "bad-mannered one."

Part of being professional is balancing politeness and friendliness with boundaries. Try to be polite to everyone. However, if life happens, or there's a blowup in a forum, and you feel you can't be polite, then it's okay to simply and firmly remove yourself from the situation. We've all been there at one point in our careers. Don't let one person bring you to their level, where you'd compromise your professionalism.

To maintain a professional persona, be courteous, be kind, be compassionate—and stay true to your core values.

BUILD YOUR SKILLS

Professionalism is also about being competent and knowing your stuff. You're competent when you can get the job done—because you know how to do the job. When you start off as an editor, an indexer, or a fact-checker, you aren't all-knowing; you're still building up your skills. In fact, professionals are always building their skills—that includes veteran editors.

No one knows everything, but we can learn what we need to know to do our work at a high level. So if you're thinking about taking on a project that's not in your area of expertise or is in an area or genre you want to transition into, build your skills first: take classes, read about the topic, read works in that genre or specialty, interview people who are experts in that field, and dispel your doubts. Fill up the knowledge gap. Continuous improvement should be part of your everyday work. If you're not sure where to start, check out the webinars and classes on offer through PEN, ACES, or the EFA. And for anyone in publishing, a great first step is to learn about conscious language.

> *The quality of your work is the foundation of your reputation.*
>
> —Brittany Dowdle

RECIPROCATE WHEN POSSIBLE, SHOW GRATITUDE ALWAYS

Reciprocating kindness is a way to show your colleagues that you respect them and care about your networking relationships. If someone has passed on a potential client lead to you, make sure to show your gratitude to that colleague. If a client has hired you to proofread their work, at the end of that project, make sure to express how grateful you are that they chose you to do that work.

There are many creative ways to show gratitude; here are some of our favorites:

- Send a thank-you card.

- Like someone's content and share/retweet it, giving that person credit—it's free! (Share about a class or talk they are going to give, an article they've written, or a resource they've created. Share a photo of your client's book and mention where it can be bought.)

- Send a gift as a thank-you for a referral. In the editing world, tea, coffee, and gift certificates to bookstores are always appreciated! Be careful not to make the gift too personal. A $35 gift for a project that earned you $350 should be considered an investment in your networking relationship. The person who referred the work to you will be grateful, and will most likely refer other work if they feel appreciated.

- Leave a recommendation on someone's LinkedIn profile, or a testimonial on their website. (Again, this is another activity that takes a few minutes and doesn't cost anything.)

- Refer connections to someone else, make an introduction, or if a good opportunity comes your way, return the favor. (Again, free! *Gratis! Libre! Kostenlos!*)

IMAGE MATTERS

The saying "You only have one chance to make a first impression" couldn't be truer. Make that first impression work for you! That means curating your words, your image, your attitude, your workspace. If a client or colleague senses that you don't take care of yourself and your business, they'll assume you're not going to take care of them or their project.

Be professional in your appearance. That doesn't mean having fancy attire, but it does mean minding personal hygiene, wearing clean clothes, and respecting the fact that many clients work in traditional offices and hold certain expectations. (Note: This general advice speaks to the realities of interacting with clients and colleagues and to general ideas of what is considered "professional," but we also want to recognize that "professional" is a cultural construct that can sometimes make us feel like we have to hide who we are or change who we are to be accepted. So our advice is: Be true to yourself and put your best effort forward. The colleagues you want to associate with will appreciate who you are. The clients who will enrich your professional life will value the real you.)

When you're working, be professional in every possible way. Keep your speech mindful and respectful, even if you don't agree with people's work styles or opinions. We try to avoid discussing religion, politics, or other sensitive subjects unless they are related to the project we are working on. Many times we don't know our client or colleague's background and what they may find offensive, so we feel it's best to avoid sticky situations.

If you know you're going to be on a video call, choose your space carefully! Many of us are multitasking at home with other family members. Our spaces can be busy, but let's make sure they're tidy. Orderly spaces tell our clients a lot about us and the way we work.

If you need to take a video call or host a meeting from your phone, find a good space and prop up your phone ahead of time. If your surroundings are unconventional, that's okay. Just keep in mind that colleagues and clients expect us to be attentive, to be active listeners, and to engage with them.

RESPECT OTHER PEOPLE'S TIME, SPACE, PREFERENCES, AND PROPRIETARY INFORMATION

If you're communicating with someone new, it's a good idea to use email first. Once you begin to understand the relationship, and if you prefer, ask whether they'd like to also communicate by text, video, or phone. Don't assume, and never text someone without asking for permission to do so first.

Avoid sending urgent requests at night or on the weekends. Be mindful that people have lives outside of work and may not appreciate hearing from you during that time. If you do need help from someone during those times, then make sure your request is specific—make it easy for people to help you.

Remember, your clients and colleagues may live in different time zones than you, and your phone call or text message may come in when they're sleeping or having dinner with their family. You don't want to be the person who is texting or calling at that time. (For example, Linda lives on the West Coast and often gets text messages from clients on the East Coast who completely disregard the time zone.)

As mentioned earlier, wait to share personal information until you develop a relationship that supports that level of sharing. If you're too informal and reveal one of your shortcomings or insecurities to a client, they may be reticent to hire you for future projects. There is a space and time for everything.

Finally, as a freelancer, you know how much time and effort you've put into building your business, making contacts, developing your processes, and winning clients. While more experienced professionals are often happy to give back and share their hard-won knowledge with colleagues who are just starting out, recognize this generosity as the gift it is. And respect their boundaries; in other words, don't respond to someone's kindness by blatantly asking for their client contact list or demanding to know what they charge (and yes, it happens all the time). If you've benefited from someone's help, remember to pass the favor on. Generosity is the fabric networks are made of.

LEARN TO FAIL FORWARD

Sometimes, even with our best intentions and planning, things can go wrong. We unintentionally hurt someone through our words or actions; we make a mistake. When that happens, our practice is to stop and take a moment to reflect. We consult with a trusted colleague.

Choose our next steps wisely. And if we need to apologize, we do—because it's important to own up to our failures and our successes.

No one in our industry is perfect in their knowledge or comprehensive in their understanding. We're all learning and evolving. When we're able to understand why we're in the wrong, and then make amends, people respect us, and we're better for doing so. We all move forward together. As Crystal Shelley states in her Conscious Language Toolkit, "While intent is important in helping us decide how to craft our message, it doesn't change how our message is received." Being mindful of the other person and seeking to lift others up is a core aspect of effective networking and sharing spaces—whether real or virtual—with others.

CONCLUSION

Thank you for investing your time and energy in learning about effective networking practices with us. Our hope is that you've worked through the exercises and worksheets in this book and have emerged with a new understanding of what networking can be—and how it can help you reach your goals.

If old, stale ideas about networking were holding you back, you now have a new framework to use—one that puts you at the center of a positive, interconnected web of colleagues, clients, and future friends. In this dynamic web, your personal communication style—your comfort zone—is not something you have to overcome, but rather, it's the foundation for your signature networking style. It's your home-field advantage. And the more connections you make by leveraging your unique style, the stronger your network will become, because it will be an outgrowth of who you are—not who you think you should be in order to be a networking superstar.

And if we haven't said it enough already, remember that networking success isn't measured by the number of people you know, the size of your digital footprint, or how many LinkedIn connections or Twitter followers you have. Instead of comparing yourself to the most visible editors on social media or the most outgoing person at the latest conference, consider the network you started with—and the network you are building for yourself. Are you making connections that are helping you develop and grow your business? Do you have trusted colleagues you can talk with in private spaces, a group of fellow editors who support and encourage one another? Are you able to give back and pay it forward by helping newcomers to the profession? If your networking is helping you reach your professional goals, then it's a success. It's that simple.

Because we're all at different stages of our careers, the main portion of this book focused on the most important aspects of our approach to networking—assessing your needs, understanding the five core networking tactics, and discovering your personal networking style. We've reserved specific how-to tips and in-depth resources for the appendixes. In the following pages you'll find practical starter tips, best practices, and other tools to help you begin your networking journey. And remember, you are not alone. There is a community of editorial professionals out there just like you, waiting to be found, heard, read, and supported.

AFTERWORD

In the summer of 2019, we volunteered to codirect the Welcome Program, an outreach of the Editorial Freelancers Association's Diversity Initiative.

Through our experience with the Welcome Program (and various conferences, classes, and chapter meetings), something became apparent: networking is hard for many of us who work in the freelance editing world, and often we're not networking effectively and efficiently. In other words, our networking efforts aren't truly helping us reach our specific goals.

As we reflected on our own networking challenges and helped colleagues in the Welcome Program work through theirs, we designed a webinar to offer guidance and tools for editors like us— a resource for extroverts as well as introverts. It took us six months of research and writing before we came up with a short presentation that we felt covered the essentials that a freelance editor, proofreader, indexer, or fact-checker needed to know about establishing a good, solid network for themselves and for their business. This book is an extension of that webinar. We hope you find its practical advice useful and that it gives you an action plan to move forward with your editorial career.

Networking occurs between living, sentient beings in the midst of evolving technology and resources. We know this book is not an exhaustive analysis of what we can accomplish together, but it's a start. If you have suggestions, ideas, or corrections—or would like to continue the conversation—we'd love to hear from you at www.networkingforeditors.com/connect.

Wishing you much success!

Brittany Dowdle and Linda Ruggeri

ACKNOWLEDGMENTS

No book is ever the product of just one person. We'd like to thank the following great minds—some of whom have allowed us to use their quotes in our book and others who have, in different ways, enlightened us and motivated us to make this book happen:

The members of the EFA's Diversity Initiative and the participants of the Welcome Program

Louise Harnby (www.louiseharnbyproofreader.com)

Sophie Playle, Liminal Pages (liminalpages.com)

Kellie Hultgren, KMH Editing (www.kmhediting.com)

Sangeeta Mehta, Mehta Book Editing (www.mehtabookeditingnewyork.com)

Katharine O'Moore-Klopf, KOK Edit (www.kokedit.com)

Madeleine Vasaly, Madeleine Vasaly Editorial Services (www.madeleinevasaly.com)

Samantha Nolan, Nolan Branding (www.nolanbranding.com)

Tanya Gold (tanyagold.com)

Ebonye Gussine Wilkins, Inclusive Media Solutions, LLC (egwmedia.com)

Ricardo Stanton-Salazar (www.stanton-salazar.com)

Adaobi Obi Tulton, Serendipity23 Editorial Services (www.serendipity23editorial.com)

Ælfwine Mischler, Mischler Editorial (www.mischlereditorial.com)

Crystal Watanabe, Pikko's House (www.pikkoshouse.com)

Luis Arturo Pelayo, Spanish to Move (www.spanishtomove.com)

Cassie Armstrong, MorningStar Editing . . . the first link in Brittany's network—thank you.

You have each been such a wonderful inspiration to us as editors.

A big thank-you to the Los Angeles Public Library, the New York Public Library, and the Brooklyn Public Library.

And finally, thank you to our families, who always support and encourage us.

APPENDIX A
NETWORKING PLEDGE

NETWORKING PLEDGE

I pledge to myself, on this day,
to try to network in a meaningful way!
With every client/colleague, big or small,
I will connect with them all.
When I reach out to others and help them too,
that's the best for my business that I can do.

APPENDIX B

WEBSITE TIPS

Nowadays there are many options if you want to build your own website. You can go the DIY route, or you can hire a professional to do it for you (while you supply the content). But before you embark on building your own website, we suggest you tally up the costs involved to build one versus the costs involved in hiring someone to do it (which would allow you to focus on paid work instead).

GETTING STARTED

The basic costs involved in having a website are for

- buying your domain name and registering it (yearly fee),
- hosting cost for the server that will house your website (yearly fee),
- securing a dedicated email address (yearly fee), and
- obtaining website security protection to eliminate cyberthreats (yearly fee).

Additional, but optional, costs involve

- a subscription to a photo library for images you can use on your site,
- access to graphic design software (like Canva, or Adobe Illustrator if you have a design background),
- hiring a graphic designer to do your logo or branding,
- paid templates or themes,
- e-commerce functionality,
- paid widgets, plug-ins, or apps,
- having your website professionally reviewed for SEO or marketing, and
- accessibility testing and design

GOING THE PROFESSIONAL ROUTE

If you decide to hire a professional, here are a few things we suggest:

- Spend time on the information architecture: how your website is structured, how the pages relate to each other, which pages are truly needed, and what content isn't pertinent. Research what other editors are doing on their sites—what you like about them and what you don't, what works and what doesn't.

- Make sure your website is secure—it should have a Secure Sockets Layer (SSL) certificate, which means any data being passed between web servers is encrypted. If it's not secure, any information a user puts on your site (e.g., their email address if they sign up for your newsletter) is not protected and could be stolen.

- After your website is up and running, make sure you are given 24/7 access to the admin panel so you can edit the content yourself instead of having to email a website administrator to request changes (which can be time-consuming for both of you).

GOING THE DIY ROUTE

There are many ways to build your website, and nowadays the pricing is more affordable than it's ever been. You can build it yourself from scratch via the open-source software WordPress—used frequently by writers and bloggers—or you can easily build it through a website-building and -hosting company (with templates and drag-and-drop content features). According to CNET, the most popular and easy website-building companies are Wix, Squarespace, Weebly, GoDaddy, Duda, and Shopify (for e-commerce).

THE BASICS

Here are our top six must-haves for a successful editor's website:

1. **A clear domain name.** This is the main part of what your unique URL is going to look like and how people will find you. Don't make it too difficult or too crafty. You want something search-friendly that people can easily remember.

2. **A good landing page.** Include a picture of yourself (up to date!), your name, what genres you edit, what type of editing you specialize in, and *what problem you're going to solve for the client.*

3. **A detailed services page.** This page explains what services you offer and what each one of them entails—*in language your client can understand.* You don't have to list your fees, but consider adding a ballpark price range or referring to a professional organization's website that has suggested rates, so your client can get a better idea of the average costs for various editorial services. It's important to educate the client that editing is not a free service.

4. **A testimonials page.** This is where visitors can read quotes from clients who enjoyed working with you. If you don't have any testimonials, start gathering them now! You'd be surprised at how kind your clients can be if you just ask them for a one-line reference about your work. If you're just starting out, volunteering can be a great way to build your first few testimonials.

5. **A contact page.** Include on this page a call to action like "Let's talk!" or "Email me for a quote!" or "How can I help you today?" Include a hyperlinked email address on your contact page that, when clicked, automatically opens a new email message window. You can also include a phone number or your city and state if you choose. Some clients will prefer to hire a local editor, as opposed to an out-of-state editor in a different time zone.

6. **Social media links.** Finally, make sure the bottom of each one of your website pages has icons that link to your business social media accounts.

These are the basic building blocks for a successful website that will give you a solid foundation for networking. Once they are in place, you can add other meaningful pages and features to drive more traffic to your site and engage with your visitors:

- Create editing packages (where you combine multiple services at a discounted rate).

- List useful resources (books, websites, blog articles, YouTube videos, etc. [some of which you have created]).

- Offer a yearly/quarterly/monthly/weekly newsletter through a sign-up form.

- Host a blog with relevant content that addresses challenges your clients or peers may struggle with.

- Design a portfolio page with links to the books/papers/content you've edited.

- Curate a products page (where you sell how-to PDFs, books, or any other material you've produced).

- Install Google Analytics. (This is just for you, so you can measure your site's performance, see what is working [so you can create more of it], and what isn't.)

Before your website goes live, hire a fellow editor or propose a proofreading swap in which you review the other person's website as a trade. As editors, we can't afford to have typos, grammar errors, or links that don't work on our own websites!

It will also reduce your stress if you recognize that your website's design needs to evolve with your business, and then invest strategically so that even if you need to add pages or redesign the site organization later, you have the ability to make changes without starting from scratch. Whether you go the DIY route or hire a designer, make sure that you keep your hi-res logo files in one place, preferably in a "website" folder that also contains the graphics that you've bought, designed, or commissioned, as well as backups of the written content. Keeping your materials organized will help you avoid the anxiety that's so common when anyone says, "I need to do something about my website!"

From Linda:

I'm pretty tech savvy and like learning about new software or platforms that can assist me with my work. I chose to build my original website on WordPress because it was important for me to learn how to do it and, most of all, to have 24/7 access to it in case I wanted to update anything. It took me one week of full-time work—and watching hours of tutorials—to learn how to use WordPress effectively, to understand how to incorporate and customize the Elementor themes, to get a grasp of widgets and plug-ins (please don't ask me about this because I still don't know enough!), to create my graphics, organize photos, write content, etc., etc. It was a great experience, but it was also exhausting. However, once my website was set up, I only had to do minor monthly maintenance to keep it dynamic by adding new content or updating themes. Building your own website requires patience, determination, and more patience. When I decided to update my website, I chose to go the professional route and hire someone to do it for me. I knew that it would be a better investment of my time to focus on what I do well (editing) and let a professional designer transform my site. It was totally worth it.

From Brittany:

I have some design experience, so when I started planning a website refresh, I thought I would design it myself, as I had my first website. I use Squarespace, and when I was first starting out, I'd had no difficulty using that platform to design my site. The result was a simple, effective, and fairly good-looking online presence. But by the time I was ready to do a complete overhaul a few years later, Squarespace had evolved—as had my needs—and after spending months in frustration, I hired a website designer who helped me work out both the logic and the aesthetics for my new site. As Linda said, sometimes you can DIY it, and sometimes it's worth it to pay for professional help.

I can maintain my site on my own, but it saved me a lot of time and stress to turn the design portion over to another person. That said, no matter how perfect your website is today, you'll need to make updates as time goes on. Your ideal clients will change, your niche may narrow or shift, and you'll want to adapt to the latest website styling and best practices.

A note on safe browsing: If you have a website already, or are designing one, make sure you're offering a safe browsing experience for your potential client through encryption and authentication. This means your website will begin with HTTPS (Hypertext Transfer Protocol Secure), instead of HTTP. HTTPS protects the integrity of the communication between your website and your client's browser, so no data is intercepted.

Why does it matter? Using HTTPS protects you, your client, and the data you're exchanging (especially if you're selling a service or product directly on your site); it also ensures that your clients' computers won't block your website or warn that it's not safe—and cost you a potential client. To make sure your website is using HTTPS, contact your webhosting company and make sure you have an SSL certificate enabled on your whole site. It's literally just a click of a button, and depending on your hosting company, it may be free, or it can be purchased as an add-on.

APPENDIX C

SOCIAL MEDIA TIPS

Social media is a powerful tool in our networking practice, but many of us avoid specific platforms —or the entire social media scene. If incorporating social media into your networking plan is a "growth zone" activity for you, the following sections will help you get comfortable with the platforms other editors currently use the most. Remember, technology is a living thing and is constantly changing; what works for us today may not be useful tomorrow. New platforms and systems are bound to emerge, so we need to know what we are comfortable with and where we can be flexible.

Like all organizations, the platforms discussed below have their strengths and weaknesses, so use judgment if you choose to join them. We're listing those that have benefited us personally, because those are the ones we have experience with. Just because we list platforms here does not mean they're flawless or that we endorse them. We've learned a great deal from each one of them, and in one way or another, when used wisely, they have helped us in our own business and networking strategies.

GET STARTED WITH SOCIAL MEDIA

Facebook

Your networking efforts on Facebook will depend on whether you're trying to spend time with other editorial professionals (to learn, socialize, and stay relevant) or with potential clients (to better understand their needs, make a good impression, or show your expertise). If you already spend a lot of personal time on Facebook, then it's a natural extension of your communication style to use Facebook for networking. It can be as simple as joining some of the editing-focused groups or some genre writing groups. But it's easy to get sucked into a Facebook time warp and waste hours at a time, so we recommend joining groups either based on referrals from people you trust or after doing a certain amount of research. It doesn't help to belong to fifty groups and lurk on each one (unless you're just gathering information). To use Facebook as a networking tool, you'll want to narrow the scope based on whom you want to reach and then focus your efforts there.

When starting out in a new group, make sure to read the group rules and follow them. It's also a good idea to check out any files the group maintains on its page, as these are often resources that have been developed for the members and may answer many of your basic questions. As you acclimate to a new Facebook group, you might want to introduce yourself and then watch the group in action for a few days to get a sense of the dynamic. If you find it's not the place for you, you can leave the group, unfollow the group, or stay a member but come back another time. Groups evolve, and so do your networking efforts.

If you have a personal Facebook account, you can network under that account, but you can also create a Facebook business account and use it to interact with both colleagues and potential clients. We don't recommend using a Facebook business account in place of your website, but it can be a great addition to your overall online presence. Depending on your niche, your contacts may be heavily involved in Facebook—or not at all. As with all of your networking efforts, let your goals and the "who" you're hoping to reach guide you. With over two billion monthly users, Facebook is too vast to navigate without a compass.

If you set up a business page, you can use it to link to your blog content, celebrate wins, and offer resources for potential clients. Or maybe you show a lighter, more personal side to your business brand, posting writing-related comics. Whatever content you've designed for your other social media platforms can also be used here. But remember that with Facebook's immense reach, it's also easy for negative impressions to take off. So whether you use a personal account or a business one, keep in mind that the way you speak and conduct yourself will influence how potential clients and colleagues view you professionally.

Instagram

If you don't have an Instagram account, or you have one that you haven't used in a long time, there are a few things you should do *before* you start posting.

- Edit your profile information by adding/reviewing the following:
  - Your name (30-character limit). How do you want to be known? You don't have to use your real name, but definitely use your business name.
  - Your website.
  - Your very short bio (150-character limit). Make sure your title, profession, or area of expertise is clear.
  - Your email address.
  - Anything else that you feel is important to have (a phone number isn't necessary).
  - Pronouns (Instagram now lets you set this in your bio).

- Choose (in Settings) whether you want your profile to be public or private (public, of course, will give you more exposure).

- Choose (in Settings) whether you want to have a personal or professional account (for this book's purpose, we assume you are going for a professional business account).

Once your profile is up to date, *then* it's okay to start posting. By now, you should be clear on what type of content you're going to post.

To Post:

Open Instagram and click the plus sign. The New Post window will open.

- Choose your image, click Next.

- Choose your filter, if you need one. If not, just click Next.

- Write your caption (2,200-character limit, 30-hashtag limit).

- Tag people if it pertains to them (optional). Think about tagging authors, clients, or fellow editors. To tag, always start by using the @ sign.

- Add your location (or the location where your clients live). You can choose different cities depending on the content you're posting about.

- Choose whether to share your post on your Facebook, Twitter, or Tumblr account.

- Click the button to share.

Instagram Tips

- Video posts always get more views than static posts.

- If posting natively (from your phone), in your phone's notes, keep a few hashtag lists for topics you post about often, and copy and paste them every time you post (e.g., hashtags for memoir topics, hashtags for writing tools, hashtags for editing resources).

- Update your hashtags according to trends. (A Google search, or other Instagram posts, will reveal trends and currently used hashtags.)

- Plan your content a week or two out. Learn about creating an editorial calendar of content and use apps or programs that let you schedule your post in advance (like Hootsuite, Later, or Buffer).

- Time your posts. Keep track of when you get the most traffic, and post at those times for greater exposure. You can also choose to make your account a business one (free!) and use "Instagram Insights" to see how many accounts you've reached, the percentage of followers/nonfollowers, content interactions, website clicks, etc.

- Reply to comments people make on your posts.

- Leave positive comments on other people's posts.

- Be creative! Don't let your content get stale! And don't feel you need to be conventional!

- Don't follow people to later unfollow them.

- Always include your geotag (the location) in your post.

As we mentioned in chapter 7, here is an example of a bookstagram:

The above image was posted on Instagram and captioned like this:

Stepping into Rural Wisconsin: Grandpa Charly's Life Vignettes, from Prussia to the Midwest chapter 5, "The Road Ahead."

. Historical family memoirs bring so much meat to the table. It's surrounding yourself with old photographs, family documents, land deeds, marriage and birth records, heirlooms and memorabilia, and reconstructing your story bit by bit.

. As an author, initially you feel that's enough. But it's not. The key to making it interesting, imho, is dropping all that information into a historical context. What, at that time, was happening in the village, town, city, state, country, world? Bam! Now, the bar just got raised, and that 1932 b&w picture of two twenty-year-old girls in romper shorts in front of a brand-new Studebaker Rockne—on a farm rural Wisconsin—has a WHOLE NEW MEANING (think, Great Depression and consider shorts were frowned upon until Katharine Hepburn started wearing them in the 1930s). And yes, we're in rural Wisconsin.

. So yes, your book is about your story, but it's also about placing your story within a "larger world" story. We don't live sealed away in a thermos. Or a ravioli. We live in towns, cities, states, countries that are constantly changing and affecting the way we carry on, the decisions we make, what we buy, eat, and how we entertain ourselves.

. Are you thinking of writing your memoir and not clear how to start or move forward? Send me an email (link in bio) and let me guide you through the process.

. #memoir #FamilyMemoir #bookstagram #HistoricalMemoir #WritersOfInstagram #FirstBook #MyWritingProject #DevelopmentalEditor #LineEditor #CopyEditor #Editors #RuralLife #MidwestLife #MidwestLiving #BookstagramRetweet #WritingAtHome #BooksAboutWisconsin #WisconsinStories #ExploreWisconsin

LinkedIn

If your platform of choice is LinkedIn, there are many things you can do to make sure you're using it effectively. Don't use LinkedIn as the virtual place to indiscriminately hand out your business card (though you should never do that anyway), but think of it more like the company mixer where you get to meet and mingle with new colleagues, exchange thoughtful ideas and resources, discuss industry news, and celebrate each other's successes. LinkedIn is *that* type of hub!

Profile Page

Primary profile: This should be your first priority. Are your name and picture up to date? Did you write your headline? If you're not sure what to put here, get inspired by reading other people's headlines and then crafting your own. Are you stating what your current work position is? This is where you can mention you're a freelancer. For example, Linda's says, "Bilingual Nonfiction Editor (specializing in memoir, cookbooks, Spanish reviewing, and technical editing)." Are your city and state current? What about your industry? If you're open to new work, make sure to choose that button too.

About: This is where you showcase your strengths and "sell" your services. In other words, it's the spot on your LinkedIn profile page where your elevator pitch/flash presentation statement goes. Make sure that it's tight, it doesn't ramble, and it says what your specialty is and how you can help clients reach their goals. *Remember, clients will be looking at your profile to see whether you can solve their problems.*

Experience: This is basically your résumé. Any particularly valuable or exciting project you've worked on, or client you've worked with (and that you have permission to mention), should be posted here. State specifically what work you did for the project to highlight your skills.

Education and Volunteer Experience: Make sure you add the schools you went to, your degrees or certifications, and any volunteer work you've done. On LinkedIn, you'll be connecting with people who share your interests and industry, as well as connecting with old school acquaintances, former colleagues, teachers, or neighbors. You never know where the next job opportunity is going to come from. And as we said in chapter 9, volunteering is a networking supercharger. It shows a potential client that you have your heart in other things as well. Even if your volunteer work is completely unrelated to editing (e.g., volunteering at a food bank, helping at an animal shelter, or weeding invasive plants at your local neighborhood park), that might be just the thing that connects you to your next client, separating you from the rest and piquing your client's interest.

Posting

To post on LinkedIn, you need to be on the home page (click the Home icon at the top of the page). The first block is Start a Post, and there you can choose what type of content to post. It's straightforward. Remember, you want to add value to the life of a potential client or a colleague (try to avoid random posting and post intentionally instead). Keep in mind that LinkedIn only allows one hyperlink to be used per post, and it won't always display the hyperlink page, so you have to read the instructions on how to get it to post. If there is a colleague you'd like to mention in your post, go ahead and tag them too, as long as it's respectful and provides meaningful content to them. (For more guidance, see "Publish Articles on LinkedIn" [www.linkedin.com/help/linkedin/answer/47538/publish-articles-on-linkedin?lang=en].)

Here are some ideas that we feel are the best types of posts for LinkedIn:

- Share a link to a good article about how to solve a problem your client might be having.

- You discovered a cool new feature in Word that's underused? Share that information with a screenshot and explain how you use it.

- Celebrate a colleague's accomplishment first by commenting on their post, and then by reposting that content on your page.

- A colleague posted interesting content? Comment on that post, and take an extra step by tagging another of your contacts in the post so they can access it too (this is where you might play matchmaker and introduce two people who don't know each other but share similar interests, and who might one day collaborate with each other).
  - For example: Joy shares a post about how a book she coauthored on woodland health practices won an award from the Association of Natural Resource Extension Professionals. So, Linda congratulates Joy on the wonderful accomplishment and also tags her friend Jay, a horticulture outreach program manager for the University of Wisconsin-Madison Extension, who might be interested in the material Joy just published. Even if nothing comes of it in terms of business opportunities for either of them, Joy appreciates the referral, Jay appreciates the contact, and Linda shows that she has her network's needs in mind.

- Share a how-to video on something you're good at (e.g., how to respond to comments in Track Changes for writers or how to start building your YA style sheet).

- Share an event you're interested in attending. Ask whether anyone is going or would like to meet you there. Maybe even get a group together. While coordinating the EFA Los Angeles Chapter, Linda often posted literary events that local editors could attend, or suggested a meetup. (For example, if you'll be speaking on a panel for your editorial organization, make sure to share the link to the event on LinkedIn.)

- Ask for help. If you're starting a new project, or are looking to change the direction of your work and want suggestions, put out a call here. You'd be amazed at how much people like giving advice and sharing their resources.

- Have you added a new skill? Received a new certification? Are you offering a new service? Make sure to announce it here, and add a direct link to your website for those who want more information.

Twitter

If there was ever a succinct platform, this one is it. With a post limit of 280 characters, you really need to put some thought into what you want to say—and how to do it in such a fraction of space. Twitter is about the "now" and about being authentic and transparent (e.g., posting organic content). Build your personal feed with a healthy stream of interesting and engaging posts that you are creating yourself or retweeting from other reputable tweets.

But recognize that not everyone on Twitter is tweeting. Many users join to stay in the know and learn about what's happening in their industry. We learned from several colleagues that there are ways of using Twitter to stay informed if you're not ready to tweet. For example, take advantage of the list feature, which lets you organize your feed by creating lists. With these lists you can group Twitter accounts you want to follow—for example, YA authors you like, or university presses you would like to work with—so you'll stay informed of all of their posts without having to sift through the entire Twitter feed. It can also be helpful to use TweetDeck to organize your view of the Twitterverse. Fellow editor Madeleine Vasaly has a great post on her website titled "A No-Fear Guide to Getting Started on Twitter," which helped us understand how to use this platform in a way that works for us.

If you're ready to give Twitter a try, here are our starter recommendations.

General

- Follow your ideal clients, the people who inspire you, the people who make you laugh or bring joy to your life (because you can do business *and* have fun too!).

- Follow hashtags relevant to your work, or to your clients' projects.

- Create or join a Twitter List relevant to the group, topic, or interest you want to follow. The List feature will let you customize, organize, and prioritize the tweets you see in your timeline.

- Use self-promotion sparingly.

- Never purchase a service that offers followers.

- When necessary, report abusive accounts to Twitter (by using the Report Tweet feature).

Tweeting

- Tweet regularly and post conversationally. Some effective ways to get started are
  - Ask a question (e.g., "What is your favorite business book so far this year?").
  - Ask for suggestions (e.g., "Looking for proofreader recommendations for my client's YA novel.").
  - Ask for ideas (e.g., "How would you . . . ?").
  - Use a hashtag related to your post, particularly one your audience uses or follows (e.g., #EditingCommunity, #FreelanceEditor, #EditorQuestion, #AtHomeEditors), but in most cases use only one or two hashtags per post.

- Reply mindfully to other people's tweets.

- Reply to other people's requests for help/advice with insight and without blatantly promoting your business. Build trust and be helpful.

- Use photos or videos to complement your post (the eye is first drawn to images and then to text). Include alt text for images and subtitles for videos.

- Emoji are fine but usually not needed. Don't over-emoji, as a long list of emoji can be super annoying for people using screen readers (think: happy face, happy face, happy face, crying face, crying face, crying face, starburst, starburst, starburst, purple alien, purple alien, purple alien).

- Avoid controversial topics or threads when engaging in them could damage your business or reputation (remember, social media thrives on conflict, and abuse does happen). Walk away from those topics unless you truly need to engage with them.

- Learn how to undo a retweet.

- Learn how to engage respectfully with someone who disagrees (instead of deleting your comment).

The downside to Twitter from an editor's perspective? You can't edit your post. So if you mess up, you have to delete it and start over.

Test, learn, and test again! The data will show you which copy, creative, and tone resonates with your audience.

—Twitter for Business

APPENDIX D

ORGANIZATIONS

The following are organizations that might be a good fit for you and your interests as you build your professional network. By no means is this list exhaustive or complete. For instance, if you specialize in editing content for a specific industry, such as organic agriculture or green energy, you'll want to develop a network within those fields as well. For more ideas, visit Katharine O'Moore-Klopf's Copyeditors' Knowledge Base, which features a huge list of organizations.

GENERAL EDITORIAL

ACES: The Society for Editing
(https://aceseditors.org)

Chartered Institute of Editing and Proofreading (CIEP)
(https://www.ciep.uk)

Editors Canada
(https://www.editors.ca)

Editorial Freelancers Association (EFA)
(https://www.the-efa.org)

Institute of Professional Editors Limited (IPEd)
(https://www.iped-editors.org)

Professional Editors Network (PEN)
(https://pensite.org)

SPECIFIC INTEREST

American Christian Fiction Writers (ACFW)
(https://acfw.com)

American Medical Writers Association (AMWA)
(https://www.amwa.org)

American Society for Indexing
(https://www.asindexing.org)

American Society of Journalists and Authors (ASJA)
  (https://asja.org)

Asian American Writers' Workshop
  (https://aaww.org)

Asian Council of Science Editors
  (https://theacse.com)

Asociación Mexicana de Editores de Revistas Biomédicas (AMERBAC)
  (http://www.amerbac.org.mx)

The Authors Guild
  (https://www.authorsguild.org)

Bay Area Editors' Forum
  (http://editorsforum.org)

Black Editors & Proofreaders
  (https://blackeditorsproofreaders.com)

Black Writers Collective
  (https://blackwriters.org)

Board of Editors in the Life Sciences (BELS)
  (https://www.bels.org)

The Children's Book Council
  (https://www.cbcbooks.org)

Copyediting-L (CE-L) (forum)
  (http://www.copyediting-l.info)

Council of Science Editors (CSE)
  (https://www.councilscienceeditors.org)

The Editors Lair (forum)
  (http://www.editorslair.com)

Freelancers Union
  (https://www.freelancersunion.org)

Historical Novel Society
  (https://historicalnovelsociety.org)

Independent Book Publishers Association (IBPA)
  (https://www.ibpa-online.org/)

Indigenous Editors Association
  (https://www.indigenouseditorsassociation.com)

Mystery Writers of America
(https://mysterywriters.org)

Native American Journalists Association (NAJA)
(https://najanewsroom.com)

National Association of Independent Writers and Editors (NAIWE)
(https://naiwe.com)

NLGJA: The Association of LGBTQ Journalists
(https://www.nlgja.org)

Nonfiction Authors Association
(https://nonfictionauthorsassociation.com)

Romantic Novelist Association (RNA)
(https://romanticnovelistsassociation.org)

Sisters in Crime
(https://www.sistersincrime.org)

Society for Technical Communication (STC)
(https://www.stc.org)

Society of Children's Book Writers and Illustrators (SCBWI)
(https://www.scbwi.org)

Spanish Editors Association (SEA)
(https://spanisheditors.org)

The Poetry Foundation
(https://www.poetryfoundation.org)

The Society of Authors (UK)
(https://www2.societyofauthors.org)

The Society of Indexers (UK)
(https://www.indexers.org.uk)

Trans Journalists Association
(https://transjournalists.org)

Women Fiction Writers
(https://www.womensfictionwriters.org)

Writers Guild of America East
(https://www.wgaeast.org)

Writers Guild of America West
(https://www.wga.org)

APPENDIX E

RECOMMENDED READINGS

Throughout our editing careers, but more so when we began researching material for this book, we have bought, checked out, and borrowed paperbacks, hardcovers, audiobooks, and ebooks related to the benefits and challenges of networking. We looked for materials that would help us make wiser choices as freelancers, as well as general advice to help strengthen and expand our businesses. Here is a list of some of the books that offered not only great approaches to networking but also taught us it's possible to live a more meaningful professional and personal life by authentically connecting with others. We hope you enjoy these books just as much as we did.

And as promised throughout the workbook, we've also included online resources that may help as you explore your own networking path.

NETWORKING

Build Your Dream Network by J. Kelly Hoey

Connect First by Melanie A. Katzman

Give and Take by Adam Grant

Joy at Work by Marie Kondo and Scott Sonenshein

Networking for People Who Hate Networking by Devora Zack

Networking Magic by Rick Frishman and Jill Lublin

The Heroine's Journey by Gail Carriger

The 11 Laws of Likability by Michelle Tillis Lederman

How to Use Social Media in Your Career by Sree Sreenivasan

CHALLENGES IN NETWORKING

"Too Much Information, or Not Enough?"
   (responsiveediting.com/too-much-information-or-not-enough)

"Remote Networking as a Person of Color"
   (hbr.org/2020/09/remote-networking-as-a-person-of-color)

"Everyone Can Learn From How Marginalized Communities Use Social Media"
(onezero.medium.com/marginalized-communities-know-the-upside-of-oversharing-on
-social-media-8bee5f908197)

"Reclaiming Networking"
(embracechange.nyc/blog/reclaiming-networking)

"The Biggest Barrier to Corporate Racial Inclusion Is Your All-White Social Network"
(www.linkedin.com/pulse/biggest-barrier-corporate-racial-inclusion-your-social-tulshyan)

"Connecting without Social Capital: How Underserved Students Network Despite Barriers"
(www.insightintodiversity.com/connecting-without-social-capital-how-underserved
-students-network-despite-barriers)

ACCESSIBILITY

"'Born Accessible' Publishing"
(pensite.org/2021/05/born-accessible-publishing)

"Federal Social Media Accessibility Toolkit Hackpad"
(digital.gov/resources/federal-social-media-accessibility-toolkit-hackpad)

"Is Your Social Media Accessible to Everyone? These 9 Best Practices Can Help"
(www.shondaland.com/act/a26294966/make-your-social-media-more-accessible)

"How to Create Accessible Posts on Instagram"
(www.business2community.com/instagram/how-to-create-accessible-posts-on
-instagram-02405647)

"Inclusive Design for Social Media: Tips for Creating Accessible Channels"
(blog.hootsuite.com/inclusive-design-social-media)

"Alt Text for SEO: How to Optimize Your Images"
(ahrefs.com/blog/alt-text)

"Everything You Need to Know to Write Effective Alt Text"
(support.microsoft.com/en-us/topic/everything-you-need-to-know-to-write-effective
-alt-text-df98f884-ca3d-456c-807b-1a1fa82f5dc2)

"Start with the 7 Core Skills | Accessible U"
(accessibility.umn.edu/what-you-can-do/start-7-core-skills)

"Making Web Images Accessible to People Who Are Blind"
(consciousstyleguide.com/making-web-images-accessible-people-blind)

"Web Accessibility: What, How, and Why"
(https://www.rabbitwitharedpen.com/blog/web-accessibility-what-how-and-why)

MASTERMIND GROUPS

"7 Reasons to Join a Mastermind Group"
 (www.forbes.com/sites/chicceo/2013/10/21/7-reasons-to-join-a-mastermind-group)

"The Power of Mastermind Groups and How You Can Benefit from Them"
 (medium.com/the-post-grad-survival-guide/the-power-of-mastermind-groups-and
 -how-you-can-benefit-from-them-bf4e6eeb66e6)

GOAL SETTING

"Goal-Setting Strategies"
 (https://medium.com/swlh/goal-setting-strategies-11d8c2c8159b)

"Goal Setting: A Scientific Guide to Setting and Achieving Goals"
 (https://jamesclear.com/goal-setting)

SELF-CARE

The Self-Care Prescription by Robyn L. Gobin
 (https://www.amazon.com/Self-Care-Prescription-Solutions-Wellbeing-ebook/dp/
 B07SYB6JXC)

"Coping with Stress"
 (www.cdc.gov/violenceprevention/about/copingwith-stresstips.html)

"Stress: Coping with Life's Stressors"
 (my.clevelandclinic.org/health/articles/6392-stress-coping-with-lifes-stressors)

"7 Self-Care Tips for Creative Freelancers"
 (fairygodboss.com/articles/7-self-care-tips-for-creative-freelancers)

"5 Ways Black Female Freelancers Can Protect Their Mental Health"
 (blog.freelancersunion.org/2021/06/07/5-ways-black-female-freelancers-can-protect-their
 -mental-health)

"Stress Management"
 (www.heart.org/en/healthy-living/healthy-lifestyle/stress-management)

National Alliance on Mental Illness
 (nami.org)

NAMI HelpLine at 800-950-NAMI (6264)

National Suicide Prevention Lifeline (Lifeline) at 1-800-273-TALK (8255)

Crisis Text Line (text HELLO to 741741)

WORKSHEETS

Start Date:
_____

Main Goal:

Building-Block Goals:

👤 **Based on my networking goal(s) for this quarter, whom do I need to reach now?**

👤 **How can I use each Networking Tactic to reach them?**

Action for My Website:

Action for My Personal Communications:

Action for My Social Media:

Action for My Professional Organizations:

Action for My Volunteer Activities:

END-OF-QUARTER NETWORKING REVIEW

End Date:
_____

Progress:

CURRENT NETWORK SNAPSHOT

Date: _____

MY SMALL, TRUSTED NETWORK

My current small, trusted network is made up of the people listed below. I know I can go to them with questions, doubts, ideas, or success stories, and that I will receive their honest feedback.

PERSON	PLATFORM	INDUSTRY/SPECIALTY REPRESENTED

Questions: Whom is my network missing?
What does this tell me about my preferred platform?
Am I networking exclusively in one niche?

CURRENT NETWORK SNAPSHOT

Date: _____

MY BROAD NETWORK

My current broad network is made up of the people listed below. I may not know all of these connections personally, but they are in my orbit and help broaden my understanding and reach.

PERSON	PLATFORM	INDUSTRY/SPECIALTY REPRESENTED

Questions: Whom is my network missing?
             What does this tell me about my preferred platform?
             Am I networking exclusively in one niche?
             Is my network shallow and disjointed?

Self-Assessment Worksheet: Website

👤 Step 1: Your website

Website URL: _____

Editing services (examples: proofreading, line editing, ghostwriting, indexing):

_____

Genre/specialty (self-help, memoir, humanities textbooks, medical journals):

_____

Main site and font colors: _____

Main font styles: _____

_____

_____

_____

Images used: _____

_____

Page categories: _____

Professionalism: 1   2   3   4   5   6   7   8   9   10

Ease of navigation: _____

Call to action: _____

Ease of contact: 1   2   3   4   5   6   7   8   9   10

Editor-centric or client-centric approach? _____

Instant emotional reaction (from "I would work with this person" to "Meh" to "No way!")

1   2   3   4   5   6   7   8   9   10

Self-Assessment Worksheet: Website

Step 2: Websites for editors offering the same services in the same genre/specialty (choose five and complete the following exercise for each)

Website URL: _____

Editing services (examples: proofreading, line editing, ghostwriting, indexing):

_____

Genre/specialty (self-help, memoir, humanities textbooks, medical journals):

_____

Main site and font colors: _____

Main font styles: _____

_____

_____

_____

Images used: _____

_____

Page categories: _____

Professionalism: 1   2   3   4   5   6   7   8   9   10

Ease of navigation: _____

Call to action: _____

Ease of contact: 1   2   3   4   5   6   7   8   9   10

Editor-centric or client-centric approach? _____

Instant emotional reaction (from "I would work with this person" to "Meh" to "No way!")

     1   2   3   4   5   6   7   8   9   10

Self-Assessment Worksheet: Website

👤 Step 3: Compare and contrast

Which site do you like the most? The least? Why? _____

_____

_____

Which site is confidence inspiring? Why?

_____

_____

Which creates excitement about the prospect of working together? How?

_____

_____

What do the top two sites have in common? _____

_____

_____

What do the bottom two have in common? _____

_____

_____

How can you apply the lessons from the most engaging sites to the development or revision of your own site? _____

_____

_____

_____

_____

_____

_____

Self-Assessment Worksheet: Communication Habits

👤 General

What are your preferred communication methods (phone calls, text, email, etc.)?
_____

Does your preferred method align with your clients' and colleagues' preferences?
_____

If not, what adjustments can you make to increase your comfort level while accommodating their needs?
_____

_____

What communication habits of others do you find most frustrating (running counter to clear communication)?
_____

_____

Which of your own habits might hinder clear communication and relationship building?
_____

_____

👤 Email evaluation

Do you routinely include an addressee line ("Dear Ana," "Hi, Joy")? _____

Do you include a personal greeting? _____

How do you sign off?_____

Do you invite further discussion or signal your availability to answer questions?
_____

Are your website and social media links included in your signature?   Yes   No

Is a business tagline included in your signature?   Yes   No

Are the main professional organizations you're a member of included in your signature?   Yes   No

Are your messages long and detailed?   Yes   No

Are they as short as humanly possible?   Yes   No

Do you use bullet points to highlight specific questions needing answers?   Yes   No

Describe the general tone of your communications in three words: _____

_____

Now, randomly select five emails from your Sent box (no more than a month old).

Do your answers in the previous section match up with what you find in the actual emails? _____

Note the differences and evaluate whether adjusting your communication style might avoid misunderstandings, improve efficiency, engage your reader, encourage finding solutions, or create space for getting to know others and allowing yourself to be known as a person behind the edits.

_____

_____

_____

_____

Select a few emails from two of your contacts whose emails are consistently clear, actionable—and personable.

Apply the email evaluation questions to their emails and note the answers.

What takeaways can you apply to your own communication style? _____

_____

_____

_____

_____

_____

Self-Assessment Worksheet: Social Media Checkup

Which platforms do you have an account with?

_____

_____

_____

Which platforms do you use on a weekly basis?

_____

_____

_____

On which platform do you regularly engage with others?

_____

_____

_____

Which is your favorite platform?

_____

Which is your least favorite?

_____

How do these platforms align with the platforms your desired network members use most (revisit chapter 4, if needed)?

_____

_____

For each platform you're on, ask:

Are you successful? _____

_____

How do you define that success (number of followers/meaningful engagements/ job opportunities/feeling in the know/learning new things/forming relationships)?

_____

_____

Are you measuring your efforts and results—or just going by feel?

_____

Self-Assessment Worksheet: Professional-Organizations Comparison Tool

Organization	Location	Membership Cost	Targeted Toward	Has Educational Programs	Has Discussion List/Forum
Circle of Editors	US	$100	academic editors	yes	yes
Total Cost		$100			

Has Online Directory	Other Benefits	My Interest Level	Results	Renew
yes	mentorship program, discounts to spa resorts, coupons for loose-leaf tea	high	Was found by one client in first month. Received referral from fellow member that turned into work.	yes

Self-Assessment Worksheet: Volunteering

Previous volunteer experience

Pros: _____

Cons: _____

Your main goal and building-block goals

1. _____

2. _____

3. _____

Issues that matter to you personally

1. _____

2. _____

3. _____

Your top skills

1. _____

2. _____

3. _____

Possible groups and activities to volunteer with

1. _____   6. _____

2. _____   7. _____

3. _____   8. _____

4. _____   9. _____

5. _____   10. _____

List three to five opportunities that further at least one business goal, one issue you care about, and one of your top skills. (Choose one and commit to it for six months to one year, then reassess.)

1. _____   4. _____

2. _____   5. _____

3. _____

Self-Assessment Worksheet: Personal Networking Style

👤 **What are your *preferred* ways to network?** _____

_____

👤 **Where do you feel most comfortable?**

In-person socializing (conferences, chapter meetings, literary festivals)?

Video and phone (webinars, virtual groups, mastermind groups)?

Email?

Online discussion lists and forums?

Social media: LinkedIn, Facebook, Twitter, Pinterest?

👤 **What new way of networking would you like to try?**

_____

👤 **What type of networking is of no interest to you? (This doesn't mean no forever, just no for now.)**

_____

👤 **If you dread the idea of networking, what specific activities are you thinking of?**

_____

👤 **Describe a networking plan that focuses on your preferred networking activities and is light on the ones you don't like doing.**

_____

_____

_____

ABOUT THE AUTHORS

Brittany Dowdle is a freelance editor with over ten years' experience in the publishing industry. She has edited the work of best-selling traditionally published authors, award-winning indie authors, and international best-selling authors. Brittany graduated summa cum laude from the University of North Georgia with a degree in English. She is a founding member of the Editorial Freelancers Association's Diversity Initiative and helped design the Welcome Program, acting as its codirector in 2019–2020. Brittany lives in the north Georgia mountains with her adventurous husband, their three cats, eight chickens, and many wild neighbors of the four-legged (or winged, or finned) variety. When she's not editing, writing, or exploring in the woods, Brittany may be found reading a book in a patch of sunshine.

Linda Ruggeri is a freelance nonfiction editor, writer, and authenticity reader (Spanish/Italian) with a degree in communications and fine arts from Loyola Marymount University. Born to immigrant parents in Los Angeles, Linda is Latinx and a first-generation American. She loves to travel and has lived in Córdoba (Argentina), Naples and Salerno (Italy), Windsor (Canada), Green Lake (Wisconsin), and Torrance (California). Linda runs the Mentorship Program for PEN as well as the Welcome Program for the EFA. Besides being an editor, Linda is an avid urban gardener and baker, a writer and a mom, and would gladly trade any night out for a good nonfiction book and a fine glass of bourbon.

If you liked this book, or found it helpful, the best compliment you can give us is leaving your honest review on Amazon or Goodreads so that other editors can find it.

We are thankful you joined us on this *Networking for Freelance Editors* journey.

Made in the USA
Coppell, TX
27 November 2021

66537156R00101